Getting Back on Track

FOUNDATIONS FOR
Biblical Women's Mentoring

Jo-Anna Culy

GETTING BACK ON TRACK
Copyright © 2017 by Jo-Anna Culy

Scripture taken from the HOLY BIBLE, NEW INTERNATIONAL VERSION®. Copyright © 1973, 1978, 1984 International Bible Society. Used by permission of Zondervan. All rights reserved. • Scripture taken from The Holy Bible, English Standard Version (ESV) is adapted from the Revised Standard Version of the Bible, copyright Division of Christian Education of the National Council of the Churches of Christ in the U.S.A. All rights reserved. • Scripture taken from the New King James Version. Copyright © 1982 by Thomas Nelson, Inc. Used by permission. All rights reserved. • Scripture quotations taken from the Holy Bible, New Living Translation, copyright © 1996, 2004, 2007 by Tyndale House Foundation. Used by permission of Tyndale House Publishers, Inc., Carol Stream, Illinois 60188. All rights reserved. • Scripture quotations taken from The Message. Copyright © 1993, 1994, 1995, 1996, 2000, 2001, 2002. Used by permission of NavPress Publishing Group. • Scripture quotations taken from the NEW AMERICAN STANDARD BIBLE®, Copyright © 1960, 1962, 1963, 1968, 1971, 1972, 1973, 1975, 1977, 1995 by The Lockman Foundation. Used by permission. Scripture taken from Holy Bible, New International Version®, NIV® Copyright ©1973, 1978, 1984, 2011 by Biblica, Inc.® Used by permission. All rights reserved worldwide.

Printed in Canada

ISBN: 978-1-4866-0950-5

Word Alive Press
131 Cordite Road, Winnipeg, MB R3W 1S1
www.wordalivepress.ca

Library and Archives Canada Cataloguing in Publication

Culy, Jo-Anna, author
    Getting back on track : foundations for biblical women's mentoring / Jo-Anna Culy.

Issued in print and electronic formats.
ISBN 978-1-4866-0950-5 (paperback).--ISBN 978-1-4866-0951-2 (pdf).--
ISBN 978-1-4866-0952-9 (html).--ISBN 978-1-4866-0953-6 (epub)

    1. Christian women--Religious life. 2. Mentoring--Religious aspects--Christianity. I. Title.

BV4527.C845 2016   253.082   C2016-903220-5
                                           C2016-903221-3

TABLE OF CONTENTS

ACKNOWLEDGEMENTS

It has been a long pregnancy and challenging delivery. I started giving birth to this book many years ago as God awakened me in the wee hours of the morning to begin writing down what He had been teaching me. In fact, I wrote the words, "These are the nights of giving birth," at 2:19 a.m. on October 22, 2008. In more recent years, God has brought alongside me many midwives to offer support and bring the effort to fruition. Jenny Jeong and Madeline Ung gave generously to support this project. They, along with Brenda Williams and Karen Cornelis, were part of a pilot group that went through a rough version of some of the material in this book in the very first Women Mentoring Women Workshop offered by Cypress Hills Ministries. Since then, Brenda and Karen have helped me at workshops, acted as sounding boards, and offered me much invaluable feedback. Friend and editor May Anne Ong offered her keen eyes and experience to help with the "delivery" of this book as well. And thanks also go to the other women who participated in the pilot group—Sarah, Virginia, Anita, Maryann, Elly, Sharon, and Doris—as well as all the women who have attended workshops since then. As they have interacted with the material and shared their thoughts, my thinking has been sharpened. Through it all, the faithful prayers of many dear friends, particularly Madeline, Gracie Churchill-Browne, Carelin Penner, and my dearest friend Sandra Jinks, have borne me through as I encountered one hurdle after another in life, each of which prevented me from focusing on this project.

I also want to sincerely thank the many women who have shared life's experiences with me, and have freely and graciously given me permission to share their stories in this book. One of these women in particular merits additional mention and gratitude. Sarah Smith is a talented artist with a sweet spirit. She cheerfully came to my aid time and time again. This book would not have been the same without her generously shared gifts and expertise.

This brings me to my husband. I'm guessing that not many husbands find themselves described by the title "midwife," but I'm including mine here. Marty has been a steady support throughout this whole process, which turned out to be quite a long haul. His helpful suggestions, expertise in biblical languages, and willingness to push me to improve my work has made what you are about to read significantly better. His greatest encouragement, though, came in the form of believing that what is contained in these pages was worth the effort.

Most of all, I am thankful to God for planting the seeds that He did deep within me, and for watering, tending, and growing them. I thank Him for saving me and giving me the privilege of living life with Him.

PREFACE

Praise be to God, the Creator of the universe and my Creator,
who has so patiently borne with me all these years,
and who is still shaping me into the image of His precious Son,
so that I am increasingly looking more and more like
I actually belong in His family.

"So you are involved in women's ministry, then."
I flinched. I had never thought of it that way before, and I didn't want to agree with this pronouncement. But as I thought it over, reflecting on the very statements I had just made myself voluntarily, I realized that this summary statement made in response was accurate.

I had been asked what I do, and as I listed the various activities that filled my days and had filled my recent years, I had painted a clear picture of women's ministry. So why did I recoil at the obvious being clearly stated? Simply put, the concept that had attached itself to the words "women's ministry" in my mind over the years had been shaped by many different experiences, none of which had actually had much to do with…well, *ministry*. For example, there had been ladies' overnight stays at the local inn, craft days, chocolate fountains, fashion shows, teas, and all-day shopping sprees at outlet malls a few cities over and up the highway. After a brief foray into this world in my early twenties, during which time I learned calligraphy and made a spectacular gingerbread house, I had found myself for the most part avoiding these events. As wholesome and enjoyable as some of them were, I failed to see how these activities were *ministry*. Guest speakers were often not believers and Christian women were told not to be too direct about sharing their faith during the events. I had been unable to see how Christian line dancing or aerobics were any different than their secular counterparts; the activities were identical, and some Christian instructors at church events even used the same crass language that nonbelievers did to instruct believing dancers to move their bodies in identical ways. I had quietly left.

As I continued to reflect on what I did with my time, I realized that over the years I had invested a great deal of my energies in teaching, and a lot of this teaching had focused on women and children. This had included teaching children the Bible and biblical truths, and discipling girls and women of all ages, both individually and in small groups. Teaching women to pray, to run a home, to study the Bible, to witness, to love and submit to their husbands, to think like a believer, and to cook. Teaching…teaching…teaching…mentoring, modeling, training.

Because I loved having people in my home, I often had women of a variety of ages coming on a weekly basis for one reason or another. And any remaining pockets of time were regularly filled in by others who came for one-time visits arranged to meet various other specific needs. As we visited, these women heard what was on my heart—my concern for the unsaved, my concern for truth. If they were unsaved, they heard my concern for them and they often heard the gospel.

Invariably, these women also saw me live. They watched me fold laundry. They quickly discovered that I loved cooking and baking, and that my least favorite chore was ironing, but that I would in the end do it anyway. They saw me when things were going well and when they weren't; on good hair days and when I was sporting "frumpy-mom-hair," as one of my sons aptly called it. And in the process of it all, we shared life. Recipes, gardening, art; rides to the doctor, the grocery store, the airport, a local nursing home. We cooked together. We planned parties for birthdays and sports teams and graduations that got guests excited about sharing the gospel and reaching out to others. We even saw gingerbread and calligraphy both used in ways that furthered God's kingdom. We talked about values. About God's goodness and His truth. I shared what He had been teaching me from His Word, and asked fellow believers to do the same. We ministered together, holding services at care facilities, visiting in hospitals, doing children's outreach in needy neighborhoods. We shared and prayed about issues facing our own children and their schools, shared comments these precious children had made during family devotions, shared their struggles and their joys. Our children grew up and left home. Still the sharing continued, about books I had read and about people I was witnessing to. Girls grew up into women and started their own families. Women came and women left. Husbands graduated or found new jobs and moved on, taking their wives with them. But still the sharing continued. Teaching, sharing, living for Jesus, intentionally focusing every day on trying to love and please God, and on laying up treasure in heaven where it lasts.

Fairly early on in this story, I had a very clear realization one day, as I was preparing to do children's outreach in a neighboring city. It was simply this: just doing the outreach was not sufficient. I had a very strong sense that if I was not also training younger ones to do the same, something significant and necessary was missing. I'm not certain if that was the true beginning point of thinking and living that way intentionally for me or not, but that same sense has continued with me to this day. Comforting a lonely older friend, visiting or praying with a hurting friend, or taking baking to the ailing parent of a friend is not enough on its own. I need to also be intentionally including others in the experience for the express purpose of whetting their appetites, alerting them to the needs and the possibilities, and training them to do the same. Including them in the process is a very natural way to accomplish these goals. And this, I believed, was one concrete expression of the biblical call to mentor. I still believe this today, but God has taught me a whole lot more about biblical mentoring since then!

As believers, we are called to be examples, to teach both content (sound doctrine) and by how we live, modeling the mature Christian life.

We are called by Jesus Himself to teach His followers to obey everything He commanded. Inspired by God, the apostle Paul described the goal this way, "to present every believer perfect in Christ" (Col. 1:28b). As those we have the privilege to help train and nurture become mature, they will begin to do the same for others as we have done for them. The cycle repeats. In this very real sense, we are called to reproduce ourselves and eventually, ultimately, to replace ourselves. Mentoring is one special means God has outlined for this process to take place, particularly among women. However, just as many things have been called "ministry" over the years, many things get called "mentoring" today.

Mentoring is not just hanging out with younger women, and it is not participating in fluffy "Christian" social events together; biblical mentoring is authentic and meaningful ministry. And it is a whole lot more besides.

INTRODUCTION:
WHO SPEAKS FOR GOD?

We had been sitting across the table exchanging hospital war stories one December evening with the young man who was staying with us. We told him about my husband Marty's botched double hernia surgery in Thailand many years ago, and how we had met old Joe Fratallenico, a fellow patient, during the long recovery time in the hospital. One afternoon after visiting Marty in his room, Joe had turned to walk out the door only to find that his hospital gown had come loose and fallen to the floor. Old Joe had found himself standing there in all his glory with a look on his face that screamed, "I get no respect!" (Thankfully, I had not been there.)

Speaking for God is no laughing matter.

Hearing this inspired our young friend across the table to tell us about his grandfather's recent hospital stay, when he had shared a room with a couple of other patients. One of these was Wally, who had suffered a stroke and could no longer speak. The other patient had taken it upon himself to serve as the voice of Wally in every conversation. Whatever the topic, this "kind" man would frequently interject what he thought Wally's view on the various matters they were discussing would be: "Well, Wally thinks such and such…Isn't that right, Wally?"

Now, I actually took many linguistics courses in my younger years, one of which required us to learn how to distinguish and write down every known sound used by humans for communication; but I am still at a loss as to how to write the sound Wally made in response to his roommate's misrepresentations of what he was thinking. Imagine the sound of someone whose mouth is taped trying to speak. "Mmm! Rrrr!" poor Wally would respond, all the while vigorously shaking his head back and forth to show his disapproval. Undeterred, his "gracious" interpreter would carry right on confidently sharing Wally's thoughts for him.

I have never met Wally; nor did I witness this interaction for myself. If I had, I probably would have had a totally different and more compassionate response. But our storyteller that December night was both humorous and talented, and we couldn't help but laugh out loud as he dramatically imitated poor Wally and his "helper."

Not many people try to speak for someone else, at least not in that person's presence. Far too many, though, seem quite willing to speak for God, and this includes the many writers and speakers who have focused on women's mentoring in recent years. Most of these would claim to provide a biblical perspective to mentoring. Sadly, however, far too many are only very loosely grounded in Scripture. As I attempt to share with you what God teaches us about women mentoring women, I approach the task with the fear of the Lord, knowing that God will hold me accountable for every word that you are about to read. Those who teach, including through books, should expect to be judged more strictly (see James 3:1). It is one thing to presume to speak for Wally; to presume to speak for the Almighty God is another matter altogether.

Although I have spent many years studying, reflecting on, and seeking to live out what you are about to read, and I believe that what follows flows out of God's Word, I still invite you to weigh each of my words against the sure Word of God. If *I* say something, you may choose whether or not to embrace it and allow it to shape your life; if *God* says something, and you claim that Jesus is your Lord, then the stakes are much higher. Ministry is only truly "ministry" if it is God's work done in God's way; and this is no less true of women's mentoring ministries. We may build huge mentoring programs using conventional wisdom and "best practices," but they will remain *our* programs rather than *God's* programs if they are not directed by God's Word.

God has revealed to us through the Scriptures how a church can become a healthy church. His ways are always best. It is critically important that we take the time to see what He has said on a given matter. The purpose of this book is to attempt to determine what God has told us about women mentoring women. It is my prayer that He will use it to help strengthen local churches by facilitating the start of biblical women's mentoring where this does not currently exist, and by helping to get women's mentoring ministries back on track where this is needed.

ALL FOR THE
GLORY OF GOD

Mentoring is one of those slippery concepts that can be hard to get a grip on. Ask any ten Christian leaders and you might get ten different definitions. Ask what mentoring looks like in practice and you'll find a vast array of quite dissimilar activities associated with this concept. This reflects the fact that "mentoring" is a fairly common word, and most people have some general ideas about what mentoring means and what is involved in mentoring someone. What are your perceptions? What would you say makes a person a mentor? How would you describe a mentor? What exactly does a mentor do? The fact that the word "mentoring" conjures up so many different ideas makes the foundation we will lay in this opening chapter particularly important.

FIRST THINGS FIRST

Like many of you, I enjoy helping others and meeting needs. I also have a bit of an adventuresome spirit and generally do not hesitate to initiate conversations with strangers. This has led to many unique opportunities over the years. I once taught a course on Debate and the Art of Argument. I had a ball! I embarked on it openly sharing that I was merely a facilitator, and intended to learn right along with those I was instructing. And that I did. One thing I learned was the importance of clearly defining key terms at the onset of the debate. This task serves two important purposes. First, it provides clarification to help ensure that everyone is on the same page; and second, it sets limits for both sides. If terms have been clearly defined at the start, the opposition cannot then utilize the strategy of altering a definition or redefining a key term mid-debate in order to undermine an argument and win points for their team.

Agreeing on a workable definition is a logical place to begin any discussion, and especially one on a topic like mentoring, which seems to mean such different things to different people. But there is an even more foundational matter that needs to be addressed first. It is the one on which we will build our study of mentoring, as well as our church mentoring programs, and our individual mentoring relationships.

IT'S ALL ABOUT GOD
You see, when you have completed this chapter and set this book down, my goal is that you take away much more than information about what mentoring is, or a feeling of excitement about mentoring, or even support, encouragement, or anticipation of the further training and equipping that, God willing, awaits you in subsequent chapters. It is my prayer that what you will take away from this chapter and this book is a sense of the awesome majesty and glory of God as revealed in mentoring. I want you to come away praising God because *He* planned this thing we call mentoring, and He prepares us and matches us with our mentees for our own good, for their good, and for His glory. He is able to make us succeed in this mission that He has called us to. Wanting each of you to go away with hearts full of praise is a big goal, but we have a big God.

With this goal in mind, we will briefly touch on a number of topics related to mentoring in this chapter, including its origins and goals, some methods for mentoring, and the qualifications of mentors. And yes, we'll spend some time looking at a definition of mentoring as well. Our treatment of each idea will be concise and introductory, but as we briefly preview each one, we want to do it all from God's perspective, working from a biblical framework, so that at the end of our time together in this chapter we will be inspired to raise our hearts to God and give Him the glory for what He has planned.

GOD'S IDEA

So where did the idea of mentoring come from? Who thought of it and what are its origins? Christian and secular authors alike often begin their discourse on mentoring with the account of a mythological character who is typically given credit as being the very first mentor. Odysseus, the main character in Homer's epic Greek poem *The Odyssey*, placed his son Telemachus in the care of a trusted friend who ended up raising him during Odysseus's long twenty-year absence. This friend's name was Mentor. This may very well be where the *word* "mentor" comes from, but the *concept* of mentoring was God's idea, and we have a record of Him sharing it with us long before Homer was even born. Although many have portrayed a number of biblical friendships as "mentoring," one of the clearest and perhaps the earliest example of mentoring is the relationship between Moses and Joshua. Moses lived around 1500 BC, and Homer wrote the Odyssey more than 700 years later. Clearly, the idea of mentoring did not originate with Homer! Moses spent around 40 years teaching, training, and shaping Joshua, and modeling for him what it looked like to effectively lead the nation of Israel. Mentoring was God's idea.

GOD'S METHOD

More than that, mentoring was, and still is, one of God's chosen methods for accomplishing his plans on earth. It is foreshadowed in Deuteronomy 6 in the instructions given to parents for raising their children. We have records of it taking place a number of times in the Old Testament (besides Moses and Joshua, Elijah and Elisha are another excellent example). It is the method Jesus used and modeled for us during His earthly ministry. It is the method God's Word repeatedly calls us to in the New Testament.

And the things you have heard me say in the presence of many witnesses entrust to reliable men who will also be qualified to teach others. (2 Tim. 2:2)

Follow the pattern of the sound words that you have heard from me, in the faith and love that are in Christ Jesus. (2 Tim. 1:13)

Simply stated, mentoring is God's idea and one of God's key methods for accomplishing some of His most important purposes.

> *The overreaching goal of mentoring is for God to receive glory.*

GOD'S GOALS

What are God's purposes for mentoring? What are His goals? There is one overarching goal that can be broken down into two parts. The key Scripture passage related to women mentoring women is found in Titus 2:

> *You must teach what is in accord with sound doctrine. ² Teach the older men to be temperate, worthy of respect, self-controlled, and sound in faith, in love and in endurance. ³ Likewise, teach the older women to be reverent in the way they live, not to be slanderers or addicted to much wine, but to teach what is good. ⁴ Then they can train the younger women to love their husbands and children, ⁵ to be self-controlled and pure, to be busy at home, to be kind, and to be subject to their husbands, so that no one will malign the word of God.* (Titus 2:1-5)

A more literal translation of the Greek will help us understand better how all of the parts of this passage fit together:

> But you, speak that which is fitting with regard to sound teaching: ² older men to be restrained/sober...³ older women, likewise, in behavior pious/devout, not slanderous, not slaves to much wine, teaching what is good, ⁴ in order that they might "train" the younger women to be those who love their

husbands, those who love their children, [5] sensible, pure, good homemakers, subject to their husbands, in order that the word of God may not be reviled.[1]

In Titus 2:3-5, God clearly calls older women to mentor or "train" younger women with the explicit goal of preventing the word of God from being reviled. Paul's use of the phrase "the word of God" almost certainly refers to the gospel rather than to the Bible here. The Greek term can mean "word," but often means "message" or a variety of other things. In this context, "message" is the most natural choice, since the

> *One way to glorify God is by guarding His reputation through living lives that prevent the gospel from being reviled.*

chapter as a whole is concerned with the gospel, which Paul refers to as "the grace of God" in 2:11 and "the blessed hope" in 2:13. In fact, the whole passage is about the gospel and behaviors that are fitting for those who have embraced it. Thus, Titus himself (2:8) and slaves who are Christians (2:9-10) must live lives worthy of the gospel for the purpose of guarding God's name from shame and making the gospel attractive. In our section, older women are to ensure that younger women live godly lives so that the gospel is not despised or disparaged.

Although it is not the explicit focus of this passage, behind all of these instructions is not only a concern for how the gospel will be perceived, but also a concern for God's own reputation. When the word of God is maligned, God Himself is maligned. God saves people for His own name's sake, for His own glory; and those who are saved are to live for His glory. This focus on God's concern for His reputation is a very common theme in Scripture.

For the sake of his great name the LORD will not reject his people, because the LORD was pleased to make you his own. (1 Sam. 12:22)

I, even I, am he who blots out your transgressions, for my own sake, and remembers your sins no more. (Isa. 43:25)

---

[1] This literal translation comes from Greek scholar Dr. Martin Culy.

But for the sake of my name I did what would keep it from being profaned in the eyes of the nations they lived among and in whose sight I had revealed myself to the Israelites by bringing them out of Egypt. (Ezek. 20:9)

In order that we, who were the first to hope in Christ, might be for the praise of his glory. (Eph. 1:12)

I am writing to you, little children, because your sins are forgiven for his name's sake. (1 John 2:12)[2]

As God's children, how we live impacts our Father's reputation. Similarly, as Marty's wife how I behave carries significant impact for his life. My behavior has the capacity to, in a very real sense, either qualify or disqualify him for the roles God wants him to play. Suppose a story of my arrest for abusing my children, or an account of my drunken brawling at a local nightclub, complete with incriminating photos, makes the front page of the weekly community newspaper. If my dear husband is pastoring a church or engaged in church planting, such behavior from me could jeopardize his ministry and livelihood. This is a powerful position to be in. Recognizing the impact that my actions can have on my husband's life, reputation, and opportunities for ministry should lead me to weigh all my actions very carefully. If I truly love my husband, I will do everything in my power to bring him honor, to help him, to build him up, and to guard his reputation.

In the very same way, each person who identifies with Christ has the potential to bring Him either honor and respect or dishonor and disrespect. It is easy to see how. If we are associated with Him, and even more than that, if we call Him our Lord and refer to ourselves as His disciples, followers, and servants, then it would be very natural for the watching world to assume that what we do and how we behave reflects His character, wishes, and values. By our words, actions, and attitudes—not to mention the activities we choose to engage in, neglect, or avoid—we can make His name famous or we can sully

---

[2] See also Josh. 7:9; Psalm 106:8; Isa. 37:35; Jer. 14:7, 21; Ezek. 20:14; Eph. 1:6, 14.

it. We are representing Him to a world that does not know Him personally.[3]

What does all of this have to do with older women mentoring younger women? Younger women are a significant group within the church, and not just in terms of numbers. They are extremely influential. As wives and mothers, they set the tone in their homes and significantly shape the next generation. In addition to that, their lives impact their husbands' reputations. Whether this large subset of the church behaves in a godly manner or not *matters*. God is very concerned with how their lives will impact the advance of the gospel and His own reputation. So, it is not surprising that He does not want them left on their own to figure things out. Instead, He has designed a good plan so that younger women can be directed, trained, and equipped to live lives worthy of the gospel. This will prevent the gospel from being reviled, and God's reputation will be guarded and upheld. This is the first part of the one overarching goal of mentoring.

The second part flows naturally from the first. Mentoring is about making disciples who are taught to obey everything Jesus commanded. "Then Jesus came to them and said, 'All authority in heaven and on earth has been given to me. Therefore go and make disciples of all nations, baptizing them in the name of the Father and of the Son and of the Holy Spirit, and teaching them to obey everything I have commanded you. And surely I am with you always, to the very end of the age'" (Matt. 28:18-20). If we claim to be Jesus' followers, we must actually *follow* Him by obeying everything He commanded, and we must teach others to do the same. In Colossians 1:28, Paul's words nicely reflect the goal of a mentor: "We proclaim him, admonishing and teaching everyone with all wisdom, *so that we may present everyone perfect in Christ.*" This statement encompasses both aspects of God's goal for mentoring, because the mature disciple, or "perfect" Christ-follower, will only bring honor to the gospel and to the Lord. Perfect Christ-followers—this is the second part of the overarching goal of mentoring.

So mentoring was God's idea; it is one of His chosen methods for accomplishing His goals. But *why* exactly does God want all of His

---

[3] 2 Cor. 5:18-20.

adopted children to look and act like His "birth Son"? Why does he want us to obey all His Son taught and to be perfect like He Himself is perfect? Quite simply, He wants this because it brings Him glory. *The overarching goal of mentoring is for God to receive glory.* Just as dishonorable living causes the gospel to be reviled by unbelievers, so honorable, transformed lives glorify God's name. Our purpose in life is to glorify God, and transformed lives that joyfully obey His commands is how He has ordained for us to do this. When a sinful life is transformed, and instead of selfish, petty, and evil responses and behaviors, we overcome evil with good, love our enemies, and look not only to our own interests but love our neighbors as we already love ourselves, this showcases the power of God to transform lives. It shows the power of His love and the extent of His grace and mercy; and as a result, His name is made glorious. Glory to God!

Mentoring serves other purposes as well. It promotes obedience to Jesus' commands, leads to reproduction in God's kingdom, and promotes exemplary Christian living. These are all encompassed in the overarching goal, bringing glory to God by producing perfect Christ-followers so that the gospel is not reviled.

QUALIFICATIONS FOR MENTORS

Now then, who can do this job? Who is qualified to serve as a mentor? And who *decides* who qualifies? Thankfully, God has not left us to our own devices, but He has a plan and He has kindly shared it with us. Several New Testament passages clearly outline what is required of mentors; some address believers broadly, and some speak specifically to us women. You know some of the things that women in particular are prone to: having too much to say, too much to eat, forgetting our predisposition to deception, not showing the proper respect to those over us, and wanting to control things ourselves; well, God addresses these for us ever so specifically in the qualifications He outlines for women mentors. He leaves no questions for us to quibble over. In Titus 2, He tells us that the older women who get to mentor must be "reverent in lifestyle." This will be evidenced by our self-control, particularly over our mouths (speech and appetites), and by our ability to teach what is good. It is a short list of qualifications, but with huge implications. And when we add to this the general requirement of being exemplary models of Christian life, we could find ourselves with *no one* who feels they are qualified to be mentors at all! But again, God comes to our rescue!

PARTNERING WITH GOD

God is our source of power. He enables, equips, and empowers us! Let's look again at Colossians 1:28, but we'll go on to verse 29 this time: "We proclaim him, admonishing and teaching everyone with all wisdom, so that we may present everyone perfect in Christ. To this end I labor, struggling with all his energy, which so powerfully works in me." Do you see the teamwork here—God and us? It is like the beautiful picture of rest Jesus painted for us when he said, "Come to me, all you who are weary and burdened, and I will give you rest. Take my yoke upon you and learn from me, for I am gentle and humble in heart, and you will find rest for your souls. For my yoke is easy and my burden is light" (Matt. 11:28-30). The yoke speaks of the work He has called us to do, but the invitation is to do it together. When we do it in His strength, in cooperation with Him, He makes the heavy yoke light. When we rely on God's strength, obedience to His commands is easy rather than a burden because He gives us both the desire to please Him and the power to do it: "for it is God who works in you to will and to act according to his good purpose" (Phil. 2:13). *God* works in us so that *we* can act according to His good purpose. And He delights to work powerfully in those who are devoted to Him: "For the eyes of the LORD range throughout the earth to strengthen those whose hearts are fully committed to him" (2 Chron. 16:9a).

The beauty of the Christian life is that it does not depend on our own strength. Jesus told Paul, "My grace is sufficient for you, for my power is made perfect in weakness" (2 Cor. 12:9), and the same is true for us. What was Paul's response to this? "Therefore I will boast all the more gladly about my weaknesses, so that Christ's power may rest on me. That is why, for Christ's sake, I delight in weaknesses, in insults, in hardships, in persecutions, in difficulties. For when I am weak, then I am strong" (2 Cor. 12:10). When we feel weak, when we recognize our inadequacies, it is at that point that we are prepared to come to Him and receive His empowering. I am not saying we are to come unprepared to the task of mentoring and expect God to miraculously snap His fingers and make us equipped to mentor. We cannot bypass the lessons that can only be learned and the maturity that can only be gained through years of experience of walking in fellowship with Christ through the challenges of life. But once that has happened we must still serve as mentors in complete dependence on God. Unless the Lord builds the house, it will most certainly be a futile building project. Confidence in the flesh and in our own competence will doom us to failure every time because God gains no glory when we do things in our own strength. I realize this is quite contrary to the thinking that is prevalent in today's milieu; but this is how it works in God's kingdom. *Everything* must be done for *His* glory. He will not share His glory with any others, not even nice Christian ladies like you and me.

When we are prepared to come to God humbly and seek His power and wisdom, the possibilities are as endless as the power He offers. Ephesians 1:19 describes this power of God that is available to help us do the work He calls us to do as "incomparably great power for us who believe." And Ephesians 3:20 reminds us that God "is able to do immeasurably more than all we ask or imagine, according to His power that is at work within us." If you are thinking about mentoring, I encourage you to read and meditate on Ephesians 1:9-23 and 3:20 so that you will have a clearer picture of the power that God makes available to His children.

SO WHAT IS MENTORING?

Although there isn't a single verse in Scripture that defines mentoring for us, there are many that describe it. Based on those, I would define mentoring as: *a person with significant maturity in the faith working with someone who is younger in the faith with the goal of helping that person to gain and apply a thorough knowledge of Scripture to all of life*. It's a relatively short and simple definition, but there's a lot of significance in each of its components.

At its core, mentoring is relational. Mentoring takes place in the context of relationships. Real mentorships are focused on people, rather than on materials. It is the person's growth and maturity that is in mind, rather than the completion of a program or a series of lessons. In fact, in mentoring it is the person's life and current circumstances—their challenges, experiences, questions, and needs—coupled with the curriculum prescribed by God in His Word that drive what is covered and discussed. Together these set the direction for the personalized "course" we call mentoring. This focus on "person over program" is a foundational distinctive of mentoring that sets it apart from typical Bible studies, book studies, and discipleship programs. In typical studies, the curriculum is set and those who are interested attend. In mentoring the needs of the individual determine what is addressed, whether that is through discussions, "studies," accountability exercises, counseling, or other means. The younger woman's needs, however, are not just determined by her, but also identified by her mentor and by God's Word. Biblical mentoring cannot simply be based on the felt needs of the one being mentored, since the human heart is prone to deception and those who are young in the faith often do not know what their real needs are. We'll come back to this issue later.

At its core, mentoring is also discipleship. Biblical mentoring is about fulfilling the Great Commission. According to Matthew 28:20, the process of making disciples involves helping individuals enter into a relationship with Christ and grow in their obedience to him. Seminary professor Howard Hendricks and his son William Hendricks are among a number of authors who attempt to distinguish between discipling and mentoring, but each of the two lists they offer actually describes *both* disciple-making *and* mentoring.[4] Alice Fryling in *Disciplemakers' Handbook* ties the two together with her proposal that "mentoring is disciple-making that is intentional, inspired, and individualized (2 Tim. 2:2)."[5] Her statement is worth considering more closely. Both mentoring and disciple-making are definitely activities that are extremely intentional

---

[4] Howard Hendricks and William Hendricks, *As Iron Sharpens Iron: Building Character in a Mentoring Relationship* (Chicago, IL: Moody, 1995), 166.

[5] Alice Fryling, *Disciplemakers' Handbook* (Downers Grove, IL: IVP, 1989), 18–19.

in nature. Check. Since the idea originated with God and it is carried out by His children in dependence on His Holy Spirit, we can also agree that in this sense it is inspired. Check. However, despite the common cultural perception or stereotype of one-on-one mentoring, there is not universal agreement that mentoring is necessarily an individualized activity, and there are actually many who both practice and would argue for the opposite. Far more importantly, Scripture does not specify that mentoring is to be carried out exclusively in one-on-one relationships, and in fact, Jesus mentored His disciples both one-on-one and in groups. So intentional and inspired, yes, but so far as mentoring being necessarily individualized, there is definitely room for various approaches.[6]

Another core element of mentoring is that it requires *an older woman*. It is noteworthy that Scripture does not advocate peer mentorship. We might even suggest that in the case of Rehoboam, Scripture illustrates the folly of peer mentoring (see 1 Kings 12:1-19). While we all learn from our peers, there is good reason to believe that the idea of peer *mentoring* came from the world. In Scripture, we are exhorted to spur one another on, certainly, but in disciple-making and mentoring there is a teacher and there is a learner; and there is no apology made for this. The teacher is to be exemplary, since it is expected that the learner, when mature, will be like the teacher. This is excellent motivation for the teacher or mentor to press on in her own sanctification!

Many have proposed that anyone can be a mentor. They simply need to find someone a little behind them in their Christian walk and start showing them the way. Helping others in this way is certainly a good and worthwhile thing to do, but it is not the model of mentoring that God designed and describes in Titus 2. Scripture actually treats leadership and training others very seriously. For now let's just say that God's choice of the words "older" and "reverent" to describe women who are qualified to mentor is what has led to the phrase "person of significant maturity in the faith" in our definition. No actual chronological age is attached to it, but the idea of maturity is clearly present. We will explore this more in Chapter 3.

---

[6] Betty Huizenga, Regi Campbell, Donna Green, Wayne Cordeiro, Linda and Anne Ortland are just a sampling of those who practice or argue for group mentoring.

COMPONENTS OF MENTORING

Some key components of mentoring found in Scripture include teaching, training, correcting, and modeling. Other aspects of mentoring include supporting, challenging, shepherding, guiding, providing accountability, rebuking, encouraging, and counseling. God is a God of great creativity and variety. Think about the members of your own family, your friends, the people you see around you in any public place (think park, airport, grocery store, or your church). Look around you at the world God has made to display His creativity, for our enjoyment, and to develop our brains as we learn about it! Our world is bursting with variety. He has given us different personalities, and gifts, and even different learning styles. He Himself teaches us using many different approaches. And this same God has given us a variety of models and many components to choose from and use in the mentoring process. In subsequent chapters we will see that biblical mentoring gives us both the freedom and the tools we need to address the vast variety of people God has made with their vast variety of challenges in the most appropriate ways. As we step out in faith to carry out His plan, He will guide each of us into the best way for us to approach each mentee—all for optimal success; all for His glory.

WHAT MENTORING IS NOT

To understand biblical mentoring, we need to not only search the Scriptures for guidance, but must also be careful to weed out those preconceived notions that do not come from Scripture. As with all other types of ministry, it is easy to mix Scripture and conventional wisdom (which sometimes comes under the label of "best practices") and produce an approach to mentoring that is quite different than what the Bible describes. So, what types of thinking do we need to guard against when we think about mentoring?

- *Mentoring is not simply imparting a body of knowledge. Instead, it is applying a thorough knowledge of Scripture to everyday life.* Knowing which Scripture passage to point a mentee to for a particular life situation requires both broad knowledge of the Word and the wisdom to know which passages are relevant and applicable. Remember the *goal* of mentoring is not information, but transformation.

• *Mentoring is not programmatic, but relational.* This is just one of the reasons why I do not typically recommend book studies as the basis of mentoring, and especially not initially. Time together should be based on biblical principles. At the same time, because there is no hard and fast biblical blueprint, schedule, or list of things that comprise a model mentoring session or relationship, it is helpful to keep some guiding principles in mind. First, whatever your approach, your time together should be firmly grounded in Scripture, and liberally watered with prayer. And second, you should make a point of always keeping the goal of mentoring clearly in view, remembering that the goal is a *person-centered one,* the perfection or maturity of your mentee, not a *program-centered one,* such as the completion of a set of materials, tasks, or exercises.

• *Mentoring is not just being a friend, even though it is at its very core relational.* If meeting for tea, visiting, and sharing about your lives is the sum total of your relationship, it is not mentoring. Friendship can indeed be a precious part of the mentoring process, but it is neither the focus nor the goal. And if friendship becomes a misplaced priority, it can actually become a hindrance to true mentoring and its goals.

• *Mentoring is not the casual influence each of us exerts on those around us, but rather it necessarily involves intentional modeling and training.* The following statements were once used to promote a mentoring program: "Mentoring is not a choice, it's a reality! Your life etches a fingerprint on the lives of others, whether you realize it or not." This is not biblical mentoring. While it is true that we all have some effect on those around us, the indirect or non-intentional influence that each human exerts on those in proximity to them is not mentoring. Mentoring is intentional shaping and training of one individual by another. Biblical mentoring has a strong correctional element to it, that of calling someone who has strayed off course back on track. It requires commitment, prayer, planning, preparation, and relationship; and it results in change, growth, and progress towards specific goals. It does not just happen.

• *Mentoring is not counseling, but it includes counseling.* The term "counseling" today commonly refers to a one-way relationship. It is one-sided in that the counselor does not typically share their own life with the client and there is not usually a sense of transparency and vulnerability on the part of the counselor. Since what is usually envisioned or referred to by the term "counseling" is ordinarily done by a professional, it is also usually quite limited in terms of the time investment that can be made, due to the costs involved. In contrast, a mentor shares her life with her mentee at a heart level. Both women embrace a level of vulnerability, and mutual trust is thus able to develop. Counseling—offering of counsel or godly, biblical advice and guidance—does occur in the mentoring relationship, but mentoring encompasses a great deal more than what is involved in a typical counseling relationship. Mentoring includes shepherding. It is walking alongside another and guiding, supporting, and encouraging her towards God-ordained goals. It is providing advice, correction, instruction, and ideas. It is being a sounding board and helping the mentee come to conclusions that she knew in her heart but had not been able to recognize or articulate. At other times it is gently revealing to her things she was *unaware* that she had in her heart. That could include good qualities, strengths, sins, or wrong motives.

• *Mentoring is not solving a mentee's problems for her, but rather helping her learn how to live responsibly and solve problems for herself.* During the course of a mentoring relationship the mentor will inevitably help the mentee solve certain problems. However, solving the mentee's problems *for* her, covering for her, or rescuing her from the consequences of her actions, her sins, or her poor choices is not mentoring. It may actually be "enabling" her. Part of a mentor's job is to help her mentee grow in wisdom, and that cannot happen if the mentee is not allowed to work through the issues she is facing and determine how Scripture speaks to them. Remember, *mentoring is all about shaping lives.* In that process, it *will* deal with the problems and issues in a mentee's life. The focus, though, is far broader.

There is much more to be said about what mentoring is and is not, but these introductory thoughts will provide the foundation for what follows, where we will flesh out what has only been introduced here.

GOD'S CURRICULUM

To recap, mentoring was God's idea. He planned this method, set the goals, outlined the qualifications for mentors, and He empowers qualified women to fulfill His purposes. Not only has God provided us with a smorgasbord of methods and approaches we can draw from and employ, but He has also provided both a generalized curriculum for all of His children, and a specialized one for training younger women. The former is found throughout His Word; the latter is found primarily in Titus 2, and is complemented by passages such as 1 Timothy 2:9-10, 1 Timothy 5:4-16, and 1 Peter 3:1-6.

GOD'S BLESSING

Finally, as icing on the cake, God gives us His blessing as we obey Him in this work. A few of the many benefits God gives to both mentor and mentee through this relationship include more intimate fellowship with Himself, deeper love for Him, a clear purpose for the mentor, guidance and support for the mentee, opportunities to lay up treasures in heaven for both, sanctification of both, and the joy of bringing God glory! This too we will explore in greater depth in the pages that follow.

CONSIDER THIS

It seems appropriate to conclude this chapter with a closing word of caution. As you study the pages that follow, you will be called to seriously consider the call to mentor younger women. Whenever a call is issued or an invitation is extended for qualified women to step forward in faith, obey God's call, and become involved in the demanding and richly rewarding life work of mentoring, we run the risk of three distinct dangers.

First, there will be women who *are* qualified to do this great work according to the requirements set by God, who will nonetheless feel inadequate and lack the confidence to step forward and rise to the challenge.

Second, there will be other women who will have more confidence than is actually warranted, and will feel like this job—that can only truly succeed by God's empowering and blessing—is doable in their own strength. For these women, the seriousness of the assignment and its responsibilities will be minimized, and they will embark on a mission they are not yet ready to handle. Biblical mentoring, however, cannot be accomplished in our own strength. It requires humility, dependence on God, and His empowering. For it to be biblical, it must also follow the pattern set out in Scripture, and God has reserved the role of mentor for those who meet certain qualifications.

Finally, we will also have to grapple with the fact that some who are qualified will feel that they are already far too busy with other commitments to mentor. When God calls us to ministry, though, answering the call usually requires sacrifice. Busy lives can and often must be de-cluttered in order to do the good works that God prepared in advance for us to do (Eph. 2:10).

I hope to address all of these concerns in what follows by helping women to gain a clearer vision of the call to mentor and of the extent of the need, and by inviting them to ask God seriously if He is calling them to do this at this point in their lives. Titus 2:3-5 does not command every older woman to become a mentor immediately, but it does urge older women to become women of godly character who will then be able to mentor younger women. For those who are willing to mentor but feel inadequate, by God's grace, through the pages of this book you will find resources that His Spirit will use to equip, encourage, and empower you. Read on, prayerfully seek God, and see how He leads you.

"Here we are as older women, God. Take us and use us for your glory. Amen!"

BIBLICAL QUALIFICATIONS
FOR MENTORING

*Likewise, teach the older women to be reverent
in the way they live,
not to be slanderers or addicted to much wine,
but to teach what is good.
Then they can train the younger women...* (Titus 2:3-4a)

*Older women, likewise, in behavior devout, not slanderers,
not slaves to much wine, teachers of what is good, in order that they
might "train" the younger women...* (literal translation)

Many questions come to mind as we begin looking more carefully at our key passages: How old is older? What about peer mentoring? What if I, as an older woman, have made serious mistakes in my life? Am I forever disqualified? What gives me the right to tell someone else how to live or what to do? What if the younger woman I am mentoring is very accomplished and successful? What if I can't answer her questions and concerns? As we take a closer look at the biblical qualifications for mentoring, our main focus will be on the character trait laid out in Titus 2. We will also discuss why God through Titus is specifically referring to *older* women, and look at some additional qualities that are worth considering in the context of mentoring. As we unpack the qualifications, we will also look at how they relate to the task of mentoring.[7]

If you are one of those readers with an eye for detail and grammar, and you added an *s* to the word "trait" in the paragraph above, I hope you used a pencil. Now is the time to erase it! That was actually not an editorial oversight; it is singular intentionally. Although it is not readily apparent in the English, there is really just one qualification for the older women in focus in verse 3. The Greek reads, "Older women, likewise, in behavior (are to be) devout." The term translated "devout" refers to one who is "devoted to a proper expression of religious beliefs"[8] and is translated "reverent" in most of our English translations. It could also be translated "pious." In the structure of the Greek text, this is the one broad qualification that is given. It is then followed by three specific examples that flesh out the qualification for us.

"IN BEHAVIOR DEVOUT"

A devout or reverent lifestyle is another way of referring to a life marked by behavior that is fitting for those who are holy. The Greek term communicates the ideas of piety, being above reproach, and having behavior that is suitable for a follower of Christ. It implies a life that is visibly different from the lives of those who are not devoted to God. In Titus 2, God is pointing to older women whose lives are *marked* by devotion to God. He is not saying that older women should be taught to do these things or behave in these ways *from time to time*. Instead, He

---

[7] We will consider how to develop these qualifications in *Staying on Track: Equipping Women for Biblical Mentoring*.

[8] Johannes P. Louw and Eugene A. Nida, eds., *Greek-English Lexicon of the New Testament Based on Semantic Domains* (2 vols. Second edition. New York: United Bible Societies, 1988, 1989), 53.6.

is making it clear that such devotion is to be woven into the very fabric of their lives. It is to represent who they are and what they are known for. This is who they are when they are with others and when they are alone. They will not be perfect, in the sense of being sinless, but they will be mature in their faith. Their lives will be exemplary because they are above reproach. Or, as the ESV puts it, such women are "reverent in the way they live."

IS PIETY GOOD OR BAD?

Piety is certainly portrayed as a positive quality in Scripture, and it has been viewed as an admirable trait historically. After all, both Scripture and people more broadly have valued those who demonstrate "a dutiful spirit of reverence for God or an earnest wish to fulfill religious obligations." More recently, though, being "pious" has taken on a negative connotation for many, with the word being used to refer to sanctimonious people who are characterized by a hypocritical concern with virtue or religious devotion. Reflection on why our language, particularly historically positive religious language, has changed in these ways would make an interesting socio-linguistic study. Why are words like "pious" or "piety" largely disdained by modern society? Whatever the reason, the eternal God of Creation, who designed the universe and all the relationships of its inhabitants, has given the quality represented by these terms great value. He esteems piety, and to please Him we must also value it and seek to develop it in our lives. Older women are to be "devout," "reverent," and "pious" in the way they live. That means they are to demonstrate their devotion to God by behavior that is fitting, appropriate, and worthy of the gospel.

"Devout," "reverent," and "pious" are not words we typically hear anymore, but they represent a concept that is common in Scripture and is described quite effectively for us in Philippians 1:27: "*Whatever* happens, conduct yourselves in a manner *worthy* of the gospel of Christ." Allow yourself a few moments to think about the scope of what God is saying here...and the difficulty. During those times when everything is going our way, living in a manner worthy of the gospel of Christ may seem possible and even reasonable; but notice how broadly this command is to impact our lives. The "whatever" at the beginning of the verse really throws a monkey wrench into our most valiant efforts to live "worthy" lives! It is there, though, to remind us of our utter dependence on the power of God. We need to be in that yoke with Jesus (Matt.

11:28-30) who empowers us to reach the very high standards He has set for us. The truth is that His standards *are* unattainable in our own strength; but as we stay connected to Him and draw strength from Him through time spent in His presence, in His Word, and in prayer, and as we abide in Him, humbly acknowledging our need for Him and asking for His help, He transforms us; and, as He does this, more and more we find ourselves responding to the "whatever" happenings in ways that are more and more consistent with the character He is developing in us. We find ourselves living in a manner that is actually *worthy* of the gospel of Christ. Our responses to challenges, trials, irritations, and even antagonism become increasingly godly. They are *fitting, suitable, and appropriate* responses for those who are children of God.

As His daughters, we are also His ambassadors to a watching world. Therefore, our increasingly godly responses bring Him glory by showcasing His power to transform sinful lives into holy ones. This is the reason that this matter of holiness, piety, and reverent living is of such great importance. It is not just because this reverent behavior is a qualification for mentoring. Our piety is also important because its effect on our lives is to be so far-reaching ("*whatever* happens"), its application to our lives is so difficult, and our living it out is so crucial for bringing glory to God and for being a testimony to unbelievers.

STAY ON TARGET

There is one final thing to consider before we look at the three specific examples of reverent behavior presented in verse 3. Unfortunately, many seeking to address the qualification of a "reverent" lifestyle have been led astray by a simple and well-intentioned practice. Perhaps you are familiar with it and will begin nodding knowingly as you read what follows. In perusing countless resources on the topic of mentoring and our passage in Titus 2, you may well imagine the vast array of proposals I came across as to what the Greek words translated "reverent in the way they live" *really* mean, and how this is to be fleshed out in our lives. Some suggested that the expression translated "reverent" by the ESV means "respectful," while others argued that the whole phrase refers to "living lives worthy of respect." One suggested a parallel between the instructions given to older men in Titus 2:2, such that as the men are to be *worthy of respect*, the women are to be known for *showing respect.* Although none of these ideas are contrary to what believers are taught to do in other places in Scripture, they completely miss the mark of what is being communicated in Titus 2:3. A lot of the confusion likely came about as a result of looking up words like "reverence," "respect," "reverent," and "respectful" in English dictionaries. Unfortunately, taking an English gloss for a Greek word, and then exploring all of the meanings of that English word has proved to be a very effective way to be thrown off the scent of the real meaning of the Greek term. Sometimes the rabbit trail can go on for an extended distance, following quite a number of diversions until the meanings that are proposed (or authoritatively stated!) have no relation at all to the meaning of the Greek word. This is truly regrettable, because when that occurs we end up miles away from the meaning that God intended to communicate.

The Greek word used in Titus 2:3 (*hieroprepeis*) does not refer to showing respect. The point is not to call for respect for others, even though elsewhere in Scripture we are clearly commanded to show proper respect to all to whom it is due.[9] Rather, the Greek term refers to showing proper reverence for God, being devout or pious in our relationship with Him, and demonstrating by our every action and attitude that we are His daughters and devoted to pleasing Him.

BUT WHY IS PIETY SO IMPORTANT?

The three concrete examples of reverent living that Paul gives to Titus are avoiding slander, avoiding drunkenness, and actively teaching what is good. The reason older women are to pursue living this sort of life is "*in order that* they may train the younger women." Having an established track record of a pious life is a prerequisite for mentoring. It is necessary if the older women are to have the desired impact on those they mentor. Thus, those who promote the idea that being a mentor simply requires a woman to be somewhat older, have some life experience, and be willing to offer a listening ear and encouragement, are not reflecting what Scripture teaches here.

---

[9] Rom. 13:7; Eph. 5:33; 6:5; 1 Thess. 5:12; 1 Tim. 6:1-2; 1 Pet. 2:17-18; 3:7, 15.

The apostle Paul shares a similar idea with his mentee, Timothy: "Watch your *life and doctrine closely*. Persevere in them, because *if* you do, you will save both yourself and your hearers" (1 Tim. 4:16). That two lettered word "if" is very significant. According to Scripture, if Timothy did not watch his life and doctrine closely, and persevere in them, he would not save himself and his hearers. Similarly, Titus 2:3-4 communicates that if your lifestyle is not reverent—that is, godly, pious, devout, and appropriate for a follower of Christ—then you are not qualified to train or mentor younger women. In order to be entrusted by God with the task of intentionally influencing others, a person must have exemplary character and a firm commitment to teaching the truth of Scripture. This is true not only of pastors and elders, but also of older women who are given the task of training younger women to follow the Lord in all areas of life.

EXEMPLARY LIVING

One result of being reverent in the way you live day in and day out is that your life becomes exemplary. Older Christians are called to live lives that are worthy of imitation. Paul told the Corinthians, "Therefore I urge you to imitate me. For this reason I am sending to you Timothy, my son whom I love, who is faithful in the Lord. He will remind you of my way of life in Christ Jesus, which agrees with what I teach everywhere in every church" (1 Cor. 4:16-17). Paul did not just teach the Corinthians that they should live exemplary lives, he lived an exemplary life himself in full view of them. After he left them, he sent Timothy, not simply to reinforce what he had taught, but also to remind them of his way of life, which was fully consistent with his teaching.

In a similar way, as we train our mentees by teaching them what is good, our lives must support our teaching. If we are teaching them to be godly, our own godliness must be evident. This does not mean that life becomes a show and we become skillful actresses. On the contrary, we must live an authentic Christian life in view of our mentees and others. We don't simply act godly in their presence, we are to *be* godly; and through our relationship and interactions, we are to allow them to see this firsthand. As our mentees are not usually with us twenty-four hours a day, they will also learn of our authentic faith and maturity through the life stories that we share with them. As they share life with us over a period of time, they will be firsthand witnesses of the transformation that is occurring in our very being through God's powerful work in us, as they observe us putting to death the flesh, obeying Him, and cooperating with what He is doing in our lives.

Elsewhere, Paul tells the Thessalonians, "You are witnesses, and so is God, of how holy, righteous and blameless we were among you who believed. For you know that we dealt with each of you as a father deals with his own children, encouraging, comforting and urging you to live lives worthy of God, who calls you into his kingdom and glory" (1 Thess. 2:10-12). "Holy, righteous and blameless living" covers all aspects of your life, independent of any other person, circumstance, or thing. Holiness is who you are when you are alone. It also includes the way that you relate to your mentee. You may be righteous and blameless in terms of avoiding blatant sin and doing many good works, but if you relate to your mentee in an impatient, unkind, or insensitive way, you are not fulfilling your role as her mentor. Likewise, if you allow her to participate in sin knowingly, without confronting her, or if you encourage her to live in a way that is not worthy of God and does not bring Him glory, then you are not blameless, and you are not fulfilling your role as her mentor.

We also see here that Paul treated those he shepherded in a fatherly manner, "encouraging, comforting, and urging them to live lives worthy of God." At times I would expect that "urging" to include instructing, warning, confronting sin, and offering correction. We must also relate to our mentees as a mother would to her own children, with tenderness and perseverance, deeply desiring their success. Many mentors become like a second mother or a spiritual mother to their mentees because of the deep heart connection that develops as both share their lives with humility and transparency, and allow their lives to be shaped by the Word of God. More than one of my mentees has called me Mom, and the huge tribute implied in this has not gone unnoticed or unappreciated. It is a gift from God. It is a blessing. It is a huge reward.

What about the times when you are not holy, righteous, and blameless? Everyone this side of heaven will sin. Even in this, though, you can still be a godly model to your mentee. If you are humble and repentant and willing to be vulnerable, God can use you to model how to handle failure and sin in a godly and exemplary manner for your mentee. Through doing this you can still be a positive role model for her. Godly remorse, confession, repentance, and purposing to persevere, receive cleansing from God, and continue moving towards the goal are traits and behaviors essential to the mature Christian life. Unfortunately, they are not commonly discussed, taught, or intentionally modeled. By your example, you can show your mentee how to humbly return to the Lord, get back on track, overcome, and even grow through the process of genuinely repenting of sin.

Exemplary living requires us to have:

1. a close and growing walk with the Lord Jesus Christ
2. willingness to work hard in complete dependence on God
3. submission to God's Spirit and will (obedience)[10]

"Whatever you have learned or received or heard from me, or seen in me—put it into practice" (Phil. 4:9). Many times the "learned, received, and heard" part is relatively easy to get right. It is the "seen" part that is more challenging. It is usually easier to teach truths than it is to live them. We can say what the proper response to a delicate situation should be for someone else, but when we find that we are thrown into a similar situation ourselves without advance notice, how do we respond? Are we able to *live* in a way that allows us to invite others to follow us? One great catalyst for exemplary living is seeking to live in constant communion with God, which the Bible describes as "abiding in Christ." Two other catalysts are getting serious about fearing God and loving God, both of which will inevitably motivate us to live to please Him. Exemplary lives will typically be an unavoidable side effect of any of these behaviors.

---

[10] One woman, Beverly, calls this an attitude of "Anywhere, anytime, anything, Lord." Carole Mayhall, *Words That Hurt, Words That Heal: Speaking the Truth in Love* (Colorado Springs, CO: NavPress, 2007), 12. Another, former missionary and popular speaker, Jean Barsness, offers herself to the Lord "Anywhere, Anytime, Any Cost" in her book with a similar title. A. Jean Barsness, *Anywhere, Anytime, Any Cost: Can I Trust God with My Zip Code* (Winnipeg, MB: Word Alive, 2013).

"Be imitators of God, therefore, as dearly loved children [2] and live a life of love, just as Christ loved us and gave himself up for us as a fragrant offering and sacrifice to God" (Eph. 5:1-2). As we grow in imitating God and reflecting His character, we will be examples for other believers to follow as they too press on, striving to be increasingly more conformed to the image of Christ. By simply living out obedience to God in the big and little things, we will help those who observe us to navigate similar hurdles, pitfalls, and challenges that they will face in their own lives.

FLESHING OUT A REVERENT LIFESTYLE

So what exactly is the reverent or pious lifestyle described in Titus 2? The three examples of piety include two behaviors to avoid and one to pursue. Both slander and being enslaved to alcohol reveal a lack of self-control. The devout woman, in contrast, will exhibit self-control broadly in her life and particularly as it pertains to her mouth. Isn't this interesting? God chose speech and appetite to highlight the need for self-control among older women. We may be tempted to smile at the stereotype of the gossiping or overly chatty female, or the one who is constantly reaching for another chocolate or coffee, or generally eating or drinking more than she needs, but lack of self-control is serious business. Without a life characterized by self-control it will be very difficult for the younger woman to respect the older woman, or to trust her judgment. Remember, one of the specific character traits older women are to teach younger women is self-control. The proverb, "Actions speak louder than words," is very applicable here. Teaching her self-control will necessitate modeling it; the alternative (commending it without practicing it yourself) constitutes hypocrisy.

"NOT TO BE SLANDERERS"

Each of the examples of reverent living is very significant for us in our roles as mentors. Naturally, a mentor is going to learn all sorts of things about her mentee in the mentoring process. It is imperative that she keep confidences. If you speak about others to your mentee, she will not trust you with her own personal issues, let alone if you are known for slandering others. Without her trust you will not be able to fulfill your role as mentor. And God forbid that you speak about her to others! If she cannot trust you, it will be difficult for you to truly help her. "A gossip betrays a confidence, but a trustworthy man keeps a secret" (Prov. 11:13). Mentors must purpose to be trustworthy.

What about those times when you need help to navigate your way through an issue your mentee is facing? If you need to get advice to know how to best shepherd her, be sure to get her permission before sharing any level of details with another person. If it is possible, aim to seek advice only from someone who has experience in the area you need help in *and* who does not know your mentee personally. Seeking out someone in a different province or state can help ensure that privacy is maintained.

Remember too that the written word is another form of the spoken word. Like the spoken word, it is an expression of who we are, our thoughts and feelings, our hopes, fears, dreams, and confessions, and our values and priorities. In today's world, it is all too easy to break confidence by means of the written word. A click of a button sends an email to those who should never have access to the information. With very little effort a confidence is broken and with it comes a breach of trust that may be extremely difficult to rebuild. Treat the written word with every bit as much care as the spoken word. Do not allow laziness about retyping something to lead you to forward an entire document that you should not. Some have inadvertently forwarded a series of interactions to a third person, who needed to see the final email but should have never seen the entire conversation. Be careful. If James were writing in the twenty-first century, he may well have said, "Be slow to speak, slow to type, and slow to forward!" along with the other admonitions of James 1:19.

My mother gave me a bit of advice early in life, which has stuck with me to this day. As I recall, I was not even old enough to have much interest in boys when she told me, "When you grow up and get married, if your husband wrongs you, do not tell anyone his faults." Her reason was simple: "Long after you have forgiven him, because you love him, the person you told, who does not love him like you do, may well remember what you said and hold it against him." Her point is well taken. Once you have spoken a word you cannot take it back, nor can you easily undo its effects. This applies to speaking about those who are not our husbands as well.

CONFIDENTIALITY

Confidentiality should not be viewed as one-sided in the mentoring relationship. The ministry of the older woman will be enhanced as she shares openly from her life experiences. Her confidences must be honored as well. The mentor is not perfect and does not pretend to be so. She should share her failures and struggles as well as what she has "mastered" in the Christian life, in each instance always keeping in mind the goal of her mentee's growth. A breach of confidence on the part of either woman can cause grave damage to the future of the relationship. Thus great care should be taken to preserve trust. Both women should treat breaches of confidence as serious and seek to avoid them at all costs. It is worth noting here that both slander and betrayal of trust surface repeatedly as major reasons why people leave the church.

A four year old boy named Billy is credited with sharing the following reflection on love: "When someone loves you, the way they say your name is different. You just know that your name is safe in their mouth."[11] This is the same assurance that those who know the godly older woman will have. They will know that their names (reputations) are safe with her. This connection between love and guarded speech is biblical: "He who covers over an offense promotes love, but whoever repeats the matter separates close friends" (Prov. 17:9). "A gossip separates close friends" (Prov. 16:28b). Remember also that "Love covers over a multitude of sins" (1 Pet. 4:8), and "It is our glory to overlook an offense" (Prov. 19:11).

Older women need to have lives that model self-control over their speech. When self-control is not exercised, it can quickly lead to gossip (inappropriately spreading information about other people) or slander (speech that casts another person in a negative light in an effort to harm their reputation). While gossip may involve spreading either true or false information, slander involves spreading information that is

---

[11] Ben Witherington, "Love --as Defined by Children." Online: http://benwitherington. blogspot.ca/2007/10/love-as-defined-by-children.html. Accessed January 3, 2016.

untrue. Slander is a form of lying. Unfortunately, it only takes one incident of slander to lose your reputation as a woman who does not slander! People instinctively seem to recall far more vividly that one conversation than a hundred others where you were discrete. The older woman who is qualified to mentor will not be a slanderer; nor will she listen to others who speak slanderously. If you have slipped into bondage to this sin, it is my prayer that God will set you free so you can eventually fulfill His purposes for you as a mentor.[12]

NOT "ADDICTED TO MUCH WINE"

Avoiding alcoholism (not being "addicted to much wine") is singled out as the second characteristic of piety for older women. If you have had any experience with those who struggle with drunkenness, you know that it almost always leads to behavior that brings shame and embarrassment. Many lives and careers have been destroyed by what people have done under the influence of alcohol (or other substances). The pastor of a church we once attended eventually had to resign due to his wife's alcoholism. For a while it was kept hidden, but after her drunkenness led to a DUI arrest that was reported in the local news, the secret was out.

Such negative consequences cannot ultimately be avoided with addictions, but they need not plague a Christian's life. Self-control is one of the fruit of the Spirit, and it is manifested in our lives more and more as we abide in Him, grow closer to Him, and yield the control of our lives and desires to Him. So, if alcohol or any other addiction is "a sin that easily besets you," it is imperative that you seek help, not only so that you can live a reverent life that pleases God, but also so that you will not be disqualified from mentoring younger women in the future.

Consistent long-term overeating can cause great harm to the one indulging in it . . . slander and drunkenness have the potential to cause great harm to others as well.

Getting help requires first taking seriously the commands of Scripture: "Do not get drunk on wine, which leads to debauchery. Instead, be

---

[12] We look at how we can partner with Him on this in *Staying on Track: Equipping Women for Biblical Mentoring*.

filled with the Spirit" (Eph. 5:18). Here we see that there is a choice to be made. Will you be controlled by some*thing* or Some*one?* Self-control can become a pattern of your life as you willingly yield your prerogative to call the shots and control your own life to God. It is self-control in that you make the choice to give the reins to Him.

"BUT TO TEACH WHAT IS GOOD"

"Teaching what is good" is the one positive expression in the short list that fleshes out what God means when He calls mentors to live lives characterized by "reverent" behavior. This is a critical prerequisite for mentors because their role centers on training younger women. However, before you disqualify yourself unnecessarily ("I could never teach the Ladies' Bible Study!"), remember that there are many ways to teach. Remember, too, that teaching skills can be learned. Acquiring teaching skills, however, is not our foremost concern. Before potential mentors consider whether they have the *ability* to teach, they must ask themselves whether they have mastered the subject matter. In order to teach, one must be well acquainted with the content she will teach. She must know her Bible well. And beyond that, she must also know how the Bible relates to everyday life. In other words, both biblical literacy and spiritual discernment (wisdom) are essential.

Let's take a closer look now at the requirements necessary for being able to teach what is good: a significant level of biblical literacy; a growing level of discernment and wisdom; and some basic teaching skills, or a willingness to develop some. And there is one additional asset that could be named as well: a mentor's growing confidence in her God-given, biblical role.

Biblical Literacy

Biblical literacy is absolutely essential for a mentor. Mentors must know their Bible well so that they know what it has to say about the issues that their mentees are facing. The goal is not to make an impression, be a know-it-all, or have a verse to rattle off whatever the occasion. Not at all. Rather, mentors must be able to teach *what is good* and to do that they need to be able to offer their mentees wise counsel that is based on Scripture. They also need to be able to use Scripture in other ways. The lists in the followings passages are not exhaustive, but simply highlight some of the many ways God's Word is designed to be used: "All Scripture is God-breathed and is useful for teaching, rebuking, correcting and training in righteousness, so that the man of God may be thoroughly equipped for every good work" (2 Tim. 3:16-17); and "Preach the Word; be prepared in season and out of season; correct, rebuke and encourage—with great patience and careful instruction" (2 Tim. 4:2).

Sound Doctrine

Like pastors and elders, mentors must have a firm grasp of sound doctrine if they are going to teach what is good. "Sound doctrine?" you ask, "Really? Aren't we making this harder than it needs to be?" I don't think so. In Titus 2:1 and 1 Timothy 4:16, Paul's mentees are instructed to "teach what is in accord with sound doctrine" and to "watch [their] life and doctrine closely." They are instructed to persevere in this. There is a reason for this and it has nothing to do with dry head knowledge. Doctrine may be broader than you realize. You probably expect that sound doctrine conforms to the gospel (1 Tim. 1:10-11), but you may be surprised to learn some of the other implications of sound doctrine for our lives.

First Timothy 1:3-9 provides the context for the verses mentioned above. Here we learn that certain behaviors are contrary to sound doctrine, reminding us that sound doctrine does not just set us right about what we should and should not believe, but it also encourages us to behave in ways that are consistent with God's laws and righteous character, and that honor the holy God who saved us through Jesus' shed blood. This is because sound doctrine shapes correct thinking, and this in turn leads to correct behavior. In this way sound doctrine encourages godliness.

Sound doctrine also leads us to have a correct view of God, and this shapes our behavior in a variety of ways. For example, if we are seeking to please God in the midst of experiencing difficulties, an accurate view of God can offer us another kind of encouragement, that is, comfort.

Whereas if we are living in rebellion or disobedience, an accurate view of God gained from sound doctrine can lead us to a proper fear of Him and repentance. Teaching sound doctrine (biblical truth) will encourage or urge us to align our lives with God's standards, character, and will. It can bring us assurance, hope, courage, and comfort from clearly understanding His person and attributes. Do you see how important sound doctrine really is? Timothy was to persevere in watching his life and doctrine closely because by doing so he would save both himself and his hearers (1 Tim. 4:16). Sound doctrine saves lives.

We do not just have to assume that the opposite is true, Scripture spells it out for us elsewhere: False doctrines promote ungodly living (1 Tim. 1:9-10). False doctrines also promote controversies and wrong thinking (2 Tim. 4:3-4; 1 Tim. 1:3-4; 6:3-4). This is why such doctrines are to be refuted and those who promote them are to be silenced by those in leadership (1 Tim. 1:3; Titus 1:9-11). As older ladies, we do not want to find ourselves in a position of needing to be refuted or silenced ourselves! For all these reasons, then, we must keep a careful watch over our doctrine. We must guard it closely, and not just with a token effort or for a brief time; we must persevere in this. Like Titus, we must "hold firmly to the trustworthy message as it has been taught, so that [we] can encourage others by sound doctrine and refute those who oppose it" (Titus 1:9). Does this mean we now need to attend seminary? No, it doesn't necessarily. It does mean, though, that we need to immerse ourselves in God's Word and allow His Holy Spirit to fulfill His role as our Teacher. If you are a clean vessel and ask Him to teach you, He will speak to your heart *through God's Word* and guide you into all truth. (We also, of course, need to submit ourselves to the teaching of godly leaders in our local church!)

I will admit that the need to be grounded in sound doctrine in order to teach what is good seemed a novel idea to me too when I first encountered it years ago,[13] but I have since come to see the benefits of this, the dangers of neglecting it, and most importantly, the biblical

---

[13] In *Becoming a Titus 2 Woman*, Martha Peace recommends that older women should be well versed in various doctrines. Martha Peace, *Becoming a Titus 2 Woman* (Bemidji, MN: Focus, 1997), 51–53.

basis for it. Can you see that the influence that has been exerted on the church from elements both without and within it does not just affect life and cultural issues, but our doctrine as well? It is for good reason that we are called to resist assimilation and renew our minds (Rom. 12:2a), and to sort through and weed out false teaching. Teaching what is good involves highlighting how the truth of Scripture differs from popular thinking in Christian circles. For far too long churches have assumed that those who have been in the church for most of their lives must have a firm grasp on doctrine, but many long-term church members cannot even give a clear explanation of the gospel. An awareness of our inadequacies should not lead us to think that we are forever disqualified if we do not yet have this knowledge. Rather, it should inspire us to grow in our knowledge of Scripture and the key doctrines of the faith. You may be surprised how easy this is to do on your own,[14] or perhaps you will prefer to gain this knowledge through sitting at the feet of someone who is well-grounded in Scripture.[15]

Certainly mentors need to be able to teach what is good in the seven target areas highlighted in Titus 2, but they also need to be able to teach what is good more broadly. They need to be able to recognize what is good and what is bad and distinguish truth from error.

Discernment and Wisdom

As a mentor listens to her mentee sharing each week, she must be able to sift through the actual words she is hearing in order to identify the concrete issues in her mentee's life that need to be addressed. Sometimes it will be necessary for a mentor to draw her mentee out and gently encourage her to open up, trust, and share more. Other times she will need to be able to identify what is irrelevant, peripheral, or superfluous in her mentee's sharing so that this information can be set aside for now and she can be freed up to get at the real heart of an issue. All of this requires wisdom.

The mentor will also need wisdom to help her bring her mentee to the place where she is willing to see for herself her need to change or to

---

[14] See *Staying on Track: Equipping Women for Biblical Mentoring.*

[15] Peace shares that the notes she prepared for teaching women's Bible Studies were reviewed by her pastor before she taught them. *Becoming a Titus 2 Woman,* 9.

work on specific areas. Again, these are all matters that need wisdom and discernment. Sometimes wisdom will lead the mentor to gently guide her mentee to arrive at a conclusion on her own. Other times she will be led to confront her directly on a sin issue. Jesus did this Himself at times, His followers followed His example, and the Scriptures command it in certain situations (Luke 11:39-54; Acts 2:34; 7:44; Matt. 18:15; Gal. 6:1). It is easy to see how wisdom fits in to being able to teach what is good! Mentors will pray for wisdom often. They will also actively pursue wisdom and discernment in other ways.

Teaching Skills

If the older woman is to teach what is good, she must also be able to teach. A formal classroom setting was likely not in the minds of either Paul or Titus when this letter was written. There are many ways to teach. If you are a pious older woman, devoted to God, chances are that you are teaching what is good to others in some way already. If you are fully convinced that you cannot teach using any approach at all, and this is what is holding you back from fulfilling the Titus 2 role, then my recommendation to you is very simple: Learn how to teach.[16]

Many Ways to Teach

Learning how to teach does not have to be overwhelming. So if, as we are discussing these prerequisites, you find yourself beginning to feel overwhelmed, please take a breather. Remember that you have an enemy who does not want you to do this; be alert to his schemes. Do not allow the evil one to intimidate you with the thought that you are not a teacher and therefore you cannot teach. Do not allow him to disqualify you that easily! Instead, consider some of the many ways in which teaching occurs. Think back to how the Holy Spirit has taught you. Many of the lessons that have really stuck have likely happened over time. Many have come through trial and error, or were impressed on your heart and mind through the sting of regret, shame, or the "school of hard knocks."

---

[16] *Staying on Track: Equipping Women for Biblical Mentoring* offers useful tools and pointers to help you begin to develop or improve some of the needed skills.

Likewise, teaching your mentee will often happen naturally over the course of many months of spending time together talking about life and how God's Word relates to the challenges of life. Teaching your mentee can be as simple as having an ordinary conversation. It can occur as you share your own experiences and the lessons you have learned. It can come about as you pray together or as she observes you in your home, in day to day public interactions, or in ministry. As you share from your own devotional reading or examples from your own life of how you are putting truths into practice and obeying your Lord, you are teaching. Teaching can also be as complex as preparing a study of a book of the Bible from scratch, or teaching your mentee specific skills, such as how to have her own personal devotional time, or how to purchase insurance, navigate the healthcare system, or manage her home. You might even be led to write your own topical Bible study for her, searching out what Scripture says clearly on a particular topic that is relevant.

Whatever the specific form your teaching takes at particular points in the mentoring relationship, it is important to remember that mentoring involves both giving instruction and setting an example. Or, put another way, it involves presenting truth and modeling the application of those truths in your own life. Second Timothy 3:14 speaks to the character of the mentor and the impact that this has on the relationship: "But as for you, continue in what you have learned and have become convinced of, because you know those from whom you learned it." Regarding modeling, 2 Timothy 1:13 says, "What you heard from me, keep as the pattern of sound teaching, with faith and love in Christ Jesus."

ABSOLUTE TRUTH

In the present age, where relativity permeates the air we breathe, there is one final note that is important to include here. There is no biblical precedent for exposing your mentee to all sorts of ideas on a topic and then letting her decide for herself what is right or wrong, true or false. Scripture unmistakably teaches that we are to pass on to others the truths of God's Word and teach the truth clearly. "If you point *these* things out to the brothers, you will be a good minister of Christ Jesus, brought up in the *truths of the faith* and of the *good teaching* that you have followed. Have *nothing* to do with godless myths and old wives' tales; rather, train yourself to be godly" (1 Tim. 4:6-7, emphasis added). Timothy is not given the freedom to come up with new or creative content. The specific truth that has been taught to him is to be the pattern he works from (2 Tim. 1:13). He is to pass it on as he received it. Call it indoctrination if you will. This is what we are called to do by God Himself…and God knows best.

Let's look at two more verses. "Command and teach *these* things" (1 Tim. 4:11, emphasis added). "And the things you have heard me say in the presence of many witnesses entrust to reliable men who will also be qualified to teach others" (2 Tim 2:2). Both of these verses contain clear instruction. Paul is saying, in essence, "What you, Timothy, received from me, Paul, in the context of my public and private teaching, you are to pass on to others who are trustworthy and who will be qualified to continue passing on that same truth." It seems likely that these men actually become qualified to teach others as a direct result of receiving the sound teaching from Timothy combined with their own trustworthy characters.

However, Paul's instructions to Timothy do not end there. He continues,

> [14] *Keep reminding God's people of these things. Warn them before God against quarreling about words; it is of no value, and only ruins those who listen.* [15] *Do your best to present yourself to God as one approved, a worker who does not need to be ashamed and who correctly handles the word of truth.* [16] *Avoid godless chatter, because those who indulge in it will become more and more ungodly.* [17] *Their teaching will spread like gangrene. Among them are Hymenaeus and Philetus,* [18] *who have departed from the truth. They say that the resurrection has already taken place, and they destroy the faith of some.* (2 Tim. 2:14-18)

Not only is Timothy to command, teach, and entrust truth to reliable men who can in turn pass it on, but he is to keep reminding them of the truths of Scripture; he is to warn them against quarreling about words; and he is to instruct them to avoid worldly, empty and foolish chatter. The reason he is to do this is because of the serious consequences that result from engaging in such talk. There is nothing more serious than wandering away from the truth (leaving the faith), and Christians today need to recognize that there are teachings floating around in Christian circles that are "destroying the faith of some." In contrast to permitting or overlooking worldly talk, Timothy is instructed to be focused on the word of truth, and to handle it properly. He is to exert himself in doing this. "Do your best" means more than making a good effort; it refers to hard work, putting your energy into the task. "Godless chatter" refers to worldly talk, and this includes the opinions of men, however esteemed, that are contrary to Scripture. Many theological tomes and blogs are filled with such talk. Rather than rendering those who feed on this fare educated and knowledgeable, God tells us that such a diet is poison; it can destroy your faith. This is why it is so necessary to avoid such talk and teachings. The Scripture actually approves of naïveté with regard to harmful teaching and ungodly behavior: "I want you to be wise about what is good, and innocent about what is evil" (Rom. 16:19b).

GROWING CONFIDENCE IN HER GOD-GIVEN, BIBLICAL ROLE

The mentor's confidence comes solely from the fact that God has assigned this particular job to godly older women. He is the One who has ordained that they have this specific role in the lives of younger women. It is, therefore, a role that older mature women need to be urged to embrace. Paul told Titus, "These, then, are the things you should teach. Encourage and rebuke with all authority. Do not let anyone despise you" (Titus 2:15). These words come at the end of the section where Titus is instructed, among other things, to teach the older women to be godly so they can "train" the younger women. The summary and exhortation in verse 15 add force to the preceding instructions and highlight the importance of the role of older women, among other things. As mentors, we can have great confidence and joy in fulfilling the assignment that God has given us. The mentor should see that because she has been called by God to do this important work, she is doing it as His emissary.

The mentor's God-given role, along with her exemplary life of devotion to God, should give her the confidence, willingness, and love that are necessary for both encouraging and admonishing her mentee.

TEACHING THE HARD LESSONS

Finally, some mentors only want to listen and encourage, and are unwilling to admonish or correct. Others wish to teach only easy topics, or discuss non-controversial issues. Mentors need to recognize that it is often touchy, delicate, or complicated subjects that require guidance from someone more mature in the faith. They must therefore be willing to address these matters. They will need to learn how to approach sensitive topics in a manner that will be well received by their mentees. They must also be willing to address the issues unwaveringly, with biblical wisdom and authority, as well as clarity, patience, gentleness, and empathy. Recalling the fact that God has assigned her role makes it easier for a mentor to perform these difficult tasks. She is not just doing this because it sounds like a good idea, but because God has asked her to do it. He has given her the authority to do this; therefore she does not need to be timid or insecure about it.

THREE ADDITIONAL QUALITIES OF A MENTOR

- *Love.* Although love is not explicitly stated in Scripture as a qualification for a mentor, the command to love other believers is so ubiquitous in God's Word that it doesn't need to be included in Titus 2. An effective mentor will love her mentee and desire to see her become "perfect" in Christ. In the mentoring relationship, the focus will be on the mentee and her growth and needs, not the needs of the mentor. If you plan to keep a record of your interaction with your mentee in a notebook (conversations, prayer requests, progress toward goals, etc.), you might want to consider writing a reminder in the front of the notebook to this effect, so that each time you meet you have a ready reminder. You could write something like, "…so that (your mentee's name) will be perfect in Christ." Or, "Depend on God; focus on (your mentee's name)."

- *Reliability.* This is a quality commended in Scripture and upheld as important for men who are being trained to be mentors/teachers. "And the things you have heard me say in the presence of many witnesses entrust to reliable men who will also be qualified to teach others" (2 Tim. 2:2). The same is true for women mentors. Two simple ways to demonstrate reliability are honoring your regularly scheduled meeting times and being punctual. Being reliable does not imply that there is no room for flexibility. In a mentoring relationship, there will be times when you (or your mentee) may have no choice but to cancel at the last minute. When this is the case, reliability entails communicating this as soon as possible. Set an example of how you want to be treated by treating her in that same way. As much as health and life permit, be a person she can count on to keep regularly agreed on meeting times and to be there for her in times of special need.

- *Commitment/Integrity.* Here, the concern is with your allegiance to your mentee, keeping your word, and persevering in the relationship. As with reliability, commitment does not imply that there is no flexibility. Different relationships have different levels of commitment. Talk about this with your mentee and come to a clear understanding of what your commitment to one another will entail. The mentoring commitment may involve several months or more than a year. Often the mentoring relationship will be more intense at first, and over time it will require less regular meetings. Your mentee will still need to know, though, that you will be there for her when she needs you. Once you have established your commitment and it has been clearly communicated and understood, you must keep it. Biblical integrity involves keeping your word even when it is inconvenient or costs you (see Psalm 15:4). One mentoring book proposes discontinuing the relationship if no progress towards the specified goals could be seen after a fixed amount of time.[17] If this is the approach you wish

---

[17] Lucibel Van Atta, *Women Encouraging Women: Who Will Disciple Me?* (Colorado Springs, CO: Multnomah, 1987), 54.

to adopt, perseverance would suggest that the time frame allotted be sufficient and reasonable. Your mentee needs to know that you are committed to her, on her side, and always seeking what is best for her.

Many others have compiled helpful lists of qualities or character traits that would be an asset for a mentor to have. Some of these are found in Appendix A.

Chapter 3

OLDER WOMEN?

Likewise, teach the older women...(Titus 2:3a)

We have already looked at the qualifications for a mentor in terms of character, but there has been one glaring omission in our discussion, which you may have noticed: The older woman must be older! So, before we move on to the question of what exactly older women are called to do, we need to answer one more foundational question: What exactly is meant by "older women"?

If the word "older" seems less than polite or flattering to you, it could be time for a different kind of makeover: a mind renewal treatment. Your discomfort with the word "older" could be an indicator that the world's toxic thinking has been slowly infiltrating your mind and causing you to see things in just the opposite way than you should. I sometimes wonder if this is a game Satan plays with us. "How can I get them to see good as evil and evil as good?"[18] Or, "How can I entice them into valuing things that are truly of little worth?" Ultimately he has so few cards to play, and yet somehow we fall for his strategies over and over and over again! I recently received a complimentary subscription to Good Housekeeping magazine. I was amazed at how few of the pages actually had anything to do with good housekeeping and how many were focused on the physical appearance of the "good housekeeper," and her seemingly tireless efforts to appear younger than she is! There were still delicious recipes, articles with tips to help the good housekeeper juggle life's demands, and the occasional heartwarming story. The challenges of age, however, were never far from the foreground. Clinging fiercely to the last fading glimmers of youth, physical fitness, and outer beauty seemed to be the ultimate goal.

CHOOSING WISELY:
A LOSING BATTLE OR GUARANTEED RETURNS

This represents an inversion of biblical values, and has often prompted me to think of Jim Elliot, martyred missionary to the Waodani Indians of South America, who said, "He is no fool who gives what he cannot keep, to gain what he cannot lose."[19] These words ultimately represented the very thing that God called him to do—lay down his physical life for the sake of bringing eternal life to those who would believe in Jesus. As a result of his sacrificial death, many Waodani eventually received the gospel and the gift of eternal life. I, however, have often thought of his statement in the context of our concept of true beauty as women. Decade after decade, century after century, many women have fallen prey to wasting the time and resources they could be investing in eternity on something that is fleeting. The Bible calls us to develop our inner character, which is the beauty that God values.[20] Like a fine wine, inner beauty has the potential to improve not just noticeably but dramatically over time. And best of all, those who invest in their inner

---

[18] This idea is found in Isaiah 5:20. See also Malachi 2:17; 3:15; Matthew 15:3-6; 23:16-23; Luke 11:35.

[19] Elisabeth Elliot, *Through Gates of Splendor* (Carol Springs, IL.: Tyndall House, 2005), 167.

[20] 1 Peter 3:2-6.

beauty are making an eternal investment. It will never fade or pass away; it cannot be stolen. It will bear eternal fruit in the form of glory to God. This is all forfeited, however, by far too many Christian women in favor of spending hours, days, and years trying to hold on to what is surely passing away,[21] through expensive products and grueling workouts.[22]

Who is wise among us? Let her prove it by a radical investment in increasing her inner beauty! Now is the time to awaken and recognize the lies the world has been feeding us. Don't drink any more worldly poison. However many changes are needed in our lives, let's be willing to pay the price. Order your life so that from here on out you are clearly investing in what is eternal. Let go of what you cannot keep anyway! Grasp firmly that which will increase in value as time goes by. Choose what will make you truly beautiful and appealing in God's eyes, and will ultimately bring Him glory.

A BAD RAP

Realistically, there are both benefits and challenges to growing older. Declining health, energy, and stamina come with age; as does the slowing of reflexes, the waning of abilities, and often the loss of memory and other mental decline. To compound things, all of this often leads to the loss of independence. It can be difficult to come to terms with the inability to do things that you once did without a second thought; and it is natural to want to postpone this process.

On the other hand, age brings with it a lifetime of experiences and memories. And the woman who has gained wisdom from these experiences will have a wealth of treasures from which to share. It is very possible for this wisdom to be gained later in life, even in retrospect, as a now-godly woman reflects over the course of her life and reevaluates the path it has taken in relation to the choices and responses she made. Her later years can be a rich time of living with dignity and honor. Again, depending on her choices, old age has the potential to bring a certain mellowing that is a very beautiful quality. Rough edges are smoothed

---

[21] Proverbs 31:30.

[22] The point is not that women should go to the opposite extreme and abandon healthy diet and exercise, personal hygiene, or all concern for their outward appearance.

off and a soft gentleness makes its appearance. There is often a greater ability to empathize, to let go of things that do not matter, to be free from the opinions of others, to be more accepting of others, and more broad-minded in a healthy, positive way. Freedom from the concern of what others think allows some older people to speak more freely and with greater urgency about matters they know are truly important. They can see more clearly that life does not go on indefinitely after all.

These sure benefits of aging, though, are often quickly forgotten as we find not only our health changing, but also our appearance! Our daily looks in the mirror bring clear reminders that the law of gravity has imposed its tyrannical rule on our poor bodies. We look flabbier, saggier, and grayer than we did just a few years ago. And our culture has conditioned us to think that all of these represent a gross injustice of this universe. In fact, for many, looking old seems to be a worse fate than actually being old. Unfortunately, youth and outward appearance have been so idolized in our culture that many of the advantages of age have been forgotten altogether. And whether it is in the church or in society at large, this attitude, coupled with the obvious vitality of youth, has often led to the myth that someone who is young will be able to do things more effectively than someone who is older. While this is certainly true in some areas of life, Titus 2 makes it clear that there are some things that older women can do that younger women are simply unable to do. So how old is "older"?

HOW OLD IS OLDER?

I have often been asked if it is truly necessary for a mentor to be chronologically older than her mentee. Although the Bible makes it clear that the mentor needs to be an "older woman," the word "older" in Titus 2 is not a comparative term that is being used to refer to one woman's age in relation to the age of another woman. Rather, it is speaking about a particular group of women within the church. Paul is instructing Titus about what he should teach older men, older women, and younger men. The older women who are taught by Titus to be devout will then be able to train the last remaining group in the church, the younger women, whom Titus is not instructed to directly teach himself.

So scripturally, the mentor clearly needs to be a woman who is "old" in terms of her age. I have sometimes explained it this way: If all the women in your church were categorized into two groups, *older* and *younger*, this would be the older group. However, although mentors will generally be older in years than their mentees, an older woman who meets the requirements described in Titus 2 is equally qualified to mentor someone who is chronologically older than she is, but is younger in terms of spiritual maturity.

So, where does that leave godly younger women? It should leave them busy serving the Lord Jesus in a broad range of other activities. They should be actively obeying Christ's call to make disciples. And they should keep working on being good disciples themselves, while they walk through life eagerly anticipating the time when they will be older women who are prepared and equipped to mentor younger women. Godly older women do not simply appear on their fiftieth birthday! They develop over time from godly younger women. Godly younger women are desperately needed in all sorts of ministry roles, but the specific, critical role of mentoring younger women described in Titus is a role given to older women.

WHY OLDER?

A good deal of mentoring necessitates that the mentor be older in years for at least a number of reasons. For one, this allows her to draw on the broad range of life experiences that are typically necessary for mentoring someone else. An experienced homemaker who has cooked for her family, her church family, or for other guests for many years will be better equipped to teach a younger woman how to manage her home well, plan a budget, or prepare nourishing meals for her husband. A wife who has been blessed

The older woman's wisdom and discernment comes not from merely living a long life, but from walking with God over time.

to celebrate her twenty- or thirty-year wedding anniversary will have a different perspective on marriage than a younger woman; and she will have a settled, established peace about her as she trains her younger mentee to love her husband, and assures her that what she is experiencing as she adjusts to married life is normal. This does not mean a mother has to have raised a large number of near-perfect, godly children in order to be qualified to mentor a young mom. Younger women can be trained by those who have learned from their mistakes as well. They can also be effectively mentored by the devout older woman who has never had a child of her own. The key is that the mentor has walked with God through the challenges of life for an extended period of time.

We began the last chapter with a discussion of the one major qualification necessary to mentor: devotion to God that is demonstrated in a reverent lifestyle. In a way, this parallels the qualifications of biblical church elders. All Christian men are called to obey all of Christ's commands, but elders are required to have a long-term reputation for such obedience. Similarly, all women are to be devout, pious, and live lives that are fitting for a believer, but older women who are called to mentor younger women must have *a proven track record* of being pious, devoted to God, and above reproach. They should be *known* for this sort of life. You should be able to ask anyone who knows this woman and have them readily corroborate that this is her undisputed reputation. While their lives will not be perfect this side of heaven, they should be exemplary.

Simply having lived longer or having had particular experiences, however, does not qualify one to offer godly advice on life's many challenges or to train a younger woman effectively in the areas that Titus 2 spells out. The older woman needs to have gained wisdom and discernment in the process. Such wisdom and discernment is absolutely necessary to mentor someone else, and this comes not from merely living a long life, but from walking with God over time. So a second reason God may have stipulated that the mentor is older is that it allows her to have gained the maturity in her relationship with Him that comes from walking with Him long-term.

To teach her mentee to persevere through trials, the mentor needs to have lived long enough to have persevered through trials herself. Perseverance is something that cannot be learned quickly! It is not a skill that can be picked up in a class or a weekend seminar. It can only be learned through personal experience, by enduring through challenges over time. I have learned more about persevering in real unconditional love through the relationships I have remained in for the long haul than I ever could have in any other way. In fact, I am not aware of any other way to learn this.

Similarly, godliness and maturity are not "skills" that can be quickly acquired through spending time with the right people. Good examples are incredibly valuable, and all believers are exhorted to seek them out and follow them, but there is no substitute for the lessons learned through your own life experiences, designed by God particularly for you. Many life experiences are designed to teach us humility. This is a defining mark of the disciple of Christ, and closely bound to devotion to God. It will mark the older woman who is privileged to be a mentor. Humility *can* be acquired and developed, but again it takes time. Even though intentionally cooperating with God can speed the process, it still requires time.

As we contemplate age and experience, a final related question is this: Does a woman have to have had a particular experience to speak to the issues related to it? Naturally, it would be very helpful if she has, particularly if she has learned the relevant lessons well, and has by God's enabling been able to glorify Him through the experience. Many older women, however, who have never been married know Scripture well and have had enough experience with those who are married to be able to offer excellent training on loving one's husband. Many single women are gifted hostesses and excellent role models for offering hospitality or managing a home. Many godly women who have never given birth or raised a child of their own can still share wisdom related to loving one's children from their knowledge of Scripture and their experience in other relationships.

You may see a picture of flexibility emerging here. There is no one profile of a perfect mentor. The important thing is for the mentor to be closely connected to God, closely "abiding in the Vine" to use Jesus' metaphor. She needs to have a solid grasp of God's Word; she needs to be saturated with it. She will then be equipped to shepherd, guide, direct, or rebuke her mentee regarding whatever issue she faces, using the powerful life-giving resource of God's Word. That Word, shared through the mentor's own life of devotion and obedience to Him, is her source of power.

We've covered a lot in these last two chapters, considering there was just one trait in Titus 2:3! If at any time you begin to feel overwhelmed by God's high calling and standard, go back and reread the sections in Chapter 1 on "Partnering with God" and the Scriptures to which they direct you. Remind yourself where the power source is. We are yoked to a mighty God!

Natalie's rough spell had been going on for an extended time. She had not been able to leave the house and was not taking any visitors. I knew. I had tried. She simply could not bring herself to answer the door. I had left flowers on the doorstep hoping they would be retrieved before they froze.

Sometime later, as I continued to reach out and pray for her, God prompted me to decorate one layer of the cake I had baked for our family to share with her. I decided to use whipped cream topped with purple sugared pansies and some bright green kiwi slices for contrast to decorate it. It then occurred to me that I might also be able to offer some encouragement in an accompanying note card. I chose some lavender colored linen cardstock left over from another project, thinking it would go nicely with the purple pansies.

She wasn't at church that evening and I hadn't expected her to be, but her husband was. I sought him out and asked if he would be able to take something home for her. I was not prepared for his reaction when he saw it, for it was only at that moment that God's plan was revealed to me. It was their wedding anniversary. And not only that, but the paper I had chosen for the note was the exact paper that they had used for their wedding invitations seven years earlier! I had had no idea. And the beautiful thing is that I hadn't needed to. I had simply been in the yoke with Jesus, doing my part as He was directing, and together with Him showing care to two of His little ones who were going through a painful time.

Chapter 4

WHAT EXACTLY
ARE MENTORS TO DO?

We have been returning to two key passages for insight regarding mentoring and disciple-making: Titus 2:2-5 and Matthew 28:19-20. The former refers to "training," at least in the NIV and ESV, while the latter focuses on teaching others to obey Jesus' commands. We have also looked at other passages that highlight the need to pass along biblical content by means of teaching, or bring about godly behaviors through modeling. In light of all of this, I originally began this chapter with the following words: "'Train' is the word God uses to describe what He intends older women to do with younger women in Titus 2; so we need to pay careful attention to it. This word sets the broad direction for women's mentoring, with everything else that we will discuss in later chapters falling under this broad umbrella term."

A FALSE START THAT WE CAN ALL LEARN FROM

The more I studied the key word in this passage, however, the more I realized that "train" does not capture what God was calling for here. Yes, the idea of training logically flows out of what Titus 2:2-5 and Matthew 28:19-20 are pointing to, but it does not do justice to the specific language that Paul chose to use. What led me to revise and leave the focus on "training" behind? How did I discover that I had veered off the path and was no longer on track? Here is what happened. I started with a false assumption that almost led me astray and this resulted in a false start in writing this chapter. I had understandably supposed that our English word "train" (Titus 2:4, NIV and ESV) had been translated from a Greek word that means "train." So, I began looking up all occurrences of the words "train," "trained," "training," and "trains" in an English concordance. I quickly accumulated quite a long list. But as I did, a growing sense that I had not done my homework was gnawing at the back of my mind. I needed to confirm which of these words actually came from the same Greek word translated "train" in Titus 2. And this was where the adventure began.

Understanding the meaning of sophronizo is pivotal to understanding the whole concept of mentoring outlined in Titus 2.

Before going any further, I have to admit that I was tempted to completely omit this section from this chapter. After all, it is quite technical, and I'm not attempting to write a commentary for scholars. Why not simply state the facts I discovered and move on? In the end, I realized that would be a mistake for a couple of reasons.

First, the meaning of the Greek word translated "train" in the NIV and ESV is extremely relevant to our upcoming discussion on approaches to mentoring. In fact, it is absolutely pivotal for a proper understanding of the concept of mentoring that is outlined in Titus 2.

Second, having been off track myself, I was sobered by the thought that I could have so easily led you astray! Many others have made the same sort of error, whether through relying on flawed assumptions, failing to do the necessary research, or just assuming that something that others have repeated in print is actually true. It is my hope that by sharing what almost led to a critical mistake on my part, I will encourage others to be more careful in their study of God's Word.

SOPHRONIZO

As I dug a little deeper into this passage, I discovered that the word translated "train" in Titus 2:4 is the Greek word *sophronizo*. It is actually a rather unusual word choice, and when a biblical author makes an unusual word choice we should take note. Allow me to explain.

In Lois Lowry's novel, *The Giver*, "precision of language" is compulsory for all in "the community." As the drama unfolds, at one point the main character, Jonas, is corrected on using the imprecise word "love," and instructed to replace it with a more precise one that would better reflect what he was actually trying to communicate. The book describes a society where, with the exception of Jonas and two others, emotions have been so suppressed that love actually no longer exists, and therefore the word previously used to convey that concept has been rendered obsolete or, in their terms, "imprecise."[23]

The point is that words are closely tied to real concepts, whether these are objects, actions, or ideas. These concepts also include emotions and idioms. Over twenty-seven years ago, during a training program, my husband and I learned to speak bits of Tok Pisin, the lingua franca of Papua New Guinea. We also learned to sing several songs in that language. To this very day, whenever I am part of a congregation singing "How Great Thou Art," I prefer to sing it in Tok Pisin. There is something incredibly simple, sincere, refreshing, and worshipful about the way the refrain was expressed in that language. Fortunately for me, or perhaps more so for those around me as I lustily sing different words than they are singing, many of the Tok Pisin words sound similar to the English ones!

My husband and I also lived in Thailand for some time many years ago. We eventually started thinking in Thai, and even dreaming in Thai; and we learned much about the culture, which is always linked to language. This means we not only thought the thoughts of our own culture using Thai words, but we also gained, to some degree, the ability

---

[23] Lois Lowry, *The Giver* (New York: Laurel Leaf, 2002).

to think like a Thai. There are many concepts that now, all these years later, we still express to one another using Thai rather than English. Why do we do this? Well, we do it because we simply do not have the same concept, or the words to express it as effectively, in English. Sometimes our expressions are idioms we have invented from Thai. When Marty says to me *puat cheewit* (literally, "life ache"), he is playing off common Thai idioms to communicate more forcefully feelings that are not so easily captured in English.

Sometimes, however, we do not reach across the globe to find expression for our thoughts and feelings. Instead, we reach back in time. I might choose to make use of a Shakespearean phrase in our conversation if I am trying to convey a concept that is no longer in existence or if modern ways of communicating the same concept seem inferior. Or perhaps I am choosing an antiquated expression precisely because I want to paint the concept itself as outdated or archaic. The point is, whenever an unusual language choice is made, we need to pause and make sure we understand the reason for the choice.

Many factors make Paul's decision to use *sophronizo* in Titus 2:4 interesting. First, this is the only place in the entire Bible where this word is used. It is used nowhere else in the Greek New Testament, and nowhere at all in the Septuagint (the Greek translation of the Old Testament that most Christians used in the first century). This is a really rare word; it was a very good thing that God prompted me to do my homework on this one! None of the many English words I looked up in my concordance had any relation to *sophronizo*.

Second, the word *sophronizo* was not commonly in use at the time that Paul wrote his letter to Titus. It was used in Classical Greek, and can be found in the writings of Euripides and Thucydides (fifth century BC) and Xenophon (fifth to fourth century BC). All of these writers wrote long before the early 60s AD when Paul wrote to Titus. In Paul's day, using this rare and apparently archaic term would likely have been very much like me greeting you with "Hark, fair maiden!" or something of that sort today!

Third, this word is not at all typical language for the concept of "training." Initial research suggested that *sophronizo* carries connotations of wise thinking. This is likely because it is related to the adjective *sophron*, a word that was still commonly used in Paul's day. *Sophron* connotes being sensible and moderate in one's behavior. It is likely this related word *sophron* that led Louw and Nida to define *sophronizo*, "to instruct someone to behave in a wise and becoming manner."[24] *Sophronizo*, however, is not a word typically used to refer to instructing, teaching, or training. Its meaning almost certainly goes far beyond that. If that is what someone wished to communicate, using *sophronizo* would not be the way to do it.

Fourth, at the same time, there were a number of other Greek words in use at the time that Paul wrote his letter that do mean "teach" or "train," but Paul chose not to use any of these. My favorite linguist and Greek scholar (my husband) has noted that Paul's decision to use this archaic word is unlikely to be inadvertent. It is simply "not the sort of thing that happens accidentally in writing." Rather than seeing this as an unusual slip of the pen or tongue, it is much more reasonable to hold that Paul made a deliberate choice, and that there would have been a particular reason for him doing so. The fact that Paul chose this unusual word rather than any of the other words that mean "train" suggests that he intended to communicate something beyond that concept. So then, what was the message?

What does this then-archaic word mean? What was Paul saying to Titus regarding the older women on the isle of Crete? The word *sophronizo* conveys the idea of calling a person back to their senses. It implies that someone is off track. It refers to the task of addressing problems, chastening the wayward individual, and wising them up. Certainly, this task may include teaching, but it will require much more than just instruction. *Sophronizo* means more than just "instructing someone to behave in a wise and becoming manner." It means correcting, addressing problems, redirecting. It is getting someone who has gotten off track back on track. It is calling someone back to their senses. There is nothing in the context that suggests a need to adopt or adapt a meaning from the related word *sophron* instead of accepting the normal meaning of the word that was actually used, *sophronizo*.

---

[24] Louw and Nida, *Greek-English Lexicon*, 33.229.

In the context of military training *sophronizo* in the Classical period carried the meaning of recalling a soldier or officer to duty.[25] This application is actually very helpful for us. A soldier in the reserves is still a soldier. It is still his identity even though he is not actively behaving like one. Similarly, there were young women in the church on Crete who were believers, but who were not actively behaving in ways that identified them as believers. They were not representing their commanding officer, God, well. They were off track in some pretty significant areas. They needed to be recalled to active duty, to live like God's daughters and representatives in this world, to be about His business. They needed to be engaged in actively bringing Him glory by their attitudes, words, and actions.

It is likely, though, that the original readers of Titus would have heard more than a military metaphor when they read this passage. Remember that Paul seems to have intentionally chosen a rare term. This alone would have made the readers stop and think about what he was saying. *Sophronizo* is closely related to another common verb, *sophroneo*. This verb is used to refer to "being in one's right mind" in Mark 5:15, Luke 8:35, and 2 Corinthians 5:13. When you take a verb like this and change the suffix to -*izo* it often means "to cause" whatever the sense of the verb stem is to come about.[26] *Sophronizo* thus likely communicates the idea of taking someone who is "out to lunch," like the demon-possessed man in Mark 5 and Luke 8, and bringing that person back to their senses. It may involve teaching, but the idea is not exactly the same. In effect, what God is saying through Paul that older women should do for younger women is to sound a wake-up call. They are to remind them of what is true in order to correct wrong thinking, get them back on track, and call them to their senses.[27] One scholar

---

[25] See Ulrich Luck, "σωφρονίζω," *TDNT*, 7:1104.

[26] As Robertson points out, this is certainly not always the case in the Koine period, but with a rare verb that is related to a common verb, using the ending to communicate a causative sense of the related verb is far more likely. A. T. Robertson, *A Grammar of the Greek New Testament in the Light of Historical Research* (Nashville: Broadman, 1934), 149, 351.

[27] My discussion of *sophronizo* is heavily dependent on the analysis of the language by Martin Culy, a recognized expert in the Greek language. His analysis, though, is supported by other experts, such as Philip H. Towner, *The Letters to Timothy and Titus* (NICNT; Grand Rapids: Eerdmans, 2006), 725; Luck, "σωφρονίζω," 1104.

even suggests that by shifting from typical teaching terminology to *sophronizo*, Paul is likely expressing the need for older women to give younger women "a figurative, sobering 'slap in the face.'"[28]

> As Winter has shown, in various settings where people (in moral and behavioral contexts) and even whole cities are in need of being "called back to their senses," Philo and Josephus (as well as Dionysius of Halicarnassus, Dio Chrysostom, and Strabo) employed *sōphronizō* in distinction from other more neutral educative terms. In the present context—given what has already emerged of the substandard Cretan values mixed in with the Christian message...understanding the verb (and therefore the nature of the teaching to be given) as a jolting "call to return to the senses" seems most suitable. The substance of the "wake-up call" is given in the seven qualities that follow.[29]

Fifth and finally, as we have begun to see, this concept of recalling a person to their senses or "wising them up" fits the context of the letter perfectly. When Paul left his mentee Titus to oversee the work in Crete and further establish the church there, things were far from in order:

> *For there are many rebellious people, mere talkers and deceivers, especially those of the circumcision group.* [11] *They must be silenced, because they are ruining whole households by teaching things they ought not to teach—and that for the sake of dishonest gain.* [12] *Even one of their own prophets has said, "Cretans are always liars, evil brutes, lazy gluttons."* [13] *This testimony is true. Therefore, rebuke them sharply, so that they will be sound in the faith* [14] *and will pay no attention to Jewish myths or to the commands of those who reject the truth.* [15] *To the pure, all things are pure, but to those who are corrupted and do not believe, nothing is pure. In fact, both their minds and consciences are corrupted.* [16] *They claim to know God,*

---

[28] Ibid., 725.
[29] Ibid., 726.

but by their actions they deny him. They are detestable, disobedient and unfit for doing anything good. (Titus 1:10-16)

What a mess! Titus was charged with bringing order to this chaos. Earlier, Paul tells Titus, "The reason I left you in Crete was that you might straighten out what was left unfinished and appoint elders in every town, as I directed you" (Titus 1:5). Refer back to verse 16 above. It seems to introduce the reason why older women, both then and now, need to call younger women to live in a manner worthy of their professed faith. If anyone claims to know God, that person's actions must be consistent with that claim (see also 1 John 2:4-6; 3:6, 9-10, 24). God, speaking through Paul, called those whose actions did not demonstrate their claim of knowing Him "detestable, disobedient and unfit for doing anything good." These are strong words. Clearly, living lives consistent with our profession of faith is serious business.

When we look at what the older women were to lead the younger women back to, we find nothing unusual. Loving one's husband and children, being kind, and so on are all things that all Christian women should be doing. It is also clear that living in these ways would bring glory to God while failure to do so would bring shame to His name. That the young women of Crete needed to be called back to obeying God in these ways is apparent by the mere fact that this passage is included in Scripture.

We saw in Titus 1:10-11 that whole households were being ruined by wrong teaching and thinking. Women are key players in all households. They typically play a key role in determining whether the household is marked by prosperity and soundness or difficulty and ruin. The wisest man who ever lived wrote, "The wise woman builds her house, but with her own hands the foolish one tears hers down" (Prov. 14:1). He also gave many examples of the effects of wisdom and folly on the prosperity of one's home. "By wisdom a house is built, and through understanding it is established; 4 through knowledge its rooms are filled with rare and beautiful treasures" (Prov. 24:3-4). This speaks of the effect a wise wife could have, while Prov. 21:9 and 19 are only two of five places that speak of one effect of a contentious wife: her behavior and attitudes motivate her husband to want to flee the home! "Better to live on a corner of the roof than share a house with a quarrelsome wife. Better to live in a desert than with a quarrelsome and ill-tempered wife" (Prov. 21:9, 19). The foolish wife who seduces other men is worse yet: "The woman Folly is loud; she is undisciplined and without knowledge. [14] She sits at the door of her house, on a seat at the highest point of the city, [15] calling out to those who pass by, who go straight on their way" (Prov. 9:13-15). Women can bring their husbands good and build them and their households up (Prov. 31:10-12; 31:31; Ruth 4:11), or they can lead them astray (1 Kings 21:25). Sadly, in the end, even Solomon was led astray by his many ungodly wives.

But a woman's influence is not limited to her own home and husband. In Scripture we see women who raised godly children that influenced whole nations, and ungodly women who wreaked havoc by their own actions and through the actions of the children they raised.[30] In these and other ways, the positions of influence that women hold extend beyond their own homes to impact the whole fabric of society. They shape and inspire generations to come, and their life choices determine much of the culture of their day as well. This all fits the context of the meaning of *sophronizo* very well. Given their positions of great influence in their homes and beyond, and the dangers the church was facing at the time this was written, it is easy to see why older women would be assigned the important task of ensuring that younger women were (or got back) on track.

STILL RELEVANT AND NEEDED

Women are still key players in all households today. They are also still being led off course by our enemy, and they still need help to live in ways that honor God. In fact, there has been such an all-out attack on Judeo-Christian values in the last half century that it could feel like this is more the case now than it has ever been before! For example, our young women today need to be called back to actually loving their husbands...

---

[30] Consider, for example, the negative influence of Jezebel on her husband Ahab and son Ahaziah, and the positive influence of Hannah on Samuel. Tracing the kings of Israel and Judah, paying attention to the mention of their mothers makes an interesting study.

rather than using, disregarding, or competing with them, or feeling like they don't even really need them. Today, many women are no longer dependent on their husbands (or fathers) to provide for them financially, and willing men are readily available for all levels of relationships with women without the commitment of marriage, further reducing the apparent "necessity" of having a husband.

Women today also need to be called back to loving their children, rather than seeing them as an inconvenience to their personal plans, goals, agendas, freedoms and even to their recreational activities! The combination of our self-centeredness and the devaluation of children cries out for an advocate for children in the form of older women who have raised children well and know the value of what they have invested their lives in. The older woman's role of urging, encouraging, and supporting young women to love their children and embrace the hard work of raising and nurturing them is just as vital today as it was in AD 60. Additionally, today's misalignment of societal values regarding children coupled with the easy access women have to technology and medicine that prevents conception or terminates newly conceived lives creates an even more basic need for many women. They now need to be encouraged to even *have* children to begin with.

What about being "subject to their husbands" (Titus 2:5)? Is there a need for women to be called back to obedience to God and submission to their own husbands today? Is this the default response of most of the younger women you know towards their husbands' leadership?

Wives are also to honor their husbands, and one expression of loving a husband (1 Cor. 13:5; Phil. 2:4) would be putting his interests above her own. If we are honest, though, we may have to admit that finding a wife today who truly honors her husband and seeks his advancement over her own is also less common than we might hope. And, like the rare gem of a woman described in Proverbs 31, a woman who wholeheartedly embraces her role as her husband's helper is still a rare find today.

What about the touchy issue of being "busy at home" or being "good homemakers"? Have many younger women today embraced this God-given assignment? Do most of the women you know today find real fulfillment in working with all their might, utilizing all the skills and gifts God has given them as they care for their homes and households? Are they content in doing this? Are they satisfied in a role that is focused on the well-being of their families? Have they been equipped to set a tone in their homes that is pleasing to God; a tone that is conducive for their husbands to lead and thrive, and for their children to be nurtured, to learn to honor their parents, and to learn to be respectful to others? Are most of the young mothers you know able to motivate, mold, and govern their children lovingly and confidently?

Today's society is unabashedly self-indulgent and hedonistic. This warrants a call back to being self-controlled and sensible. Similarly, the prevalence of promiscuity and immorality warrants a call back to purity. The need to spotlight God's standards of purity in other areas, such as speech, business dealings, or other social interactions is also very real.

The unblushing acceptance of self-centeredness would certainly lead Paul to instruct young women today to work hard at being kind rather than falling prey to the pride, arrogance, and rudeness that accompanies the "I'm on my way to the top and you are likely to be crushed if you get in my way" mindset. Such behavior does not partner well with compassion, politeness, sympathy, forgiveness, or any of the other facets of kindness. And it does not show the watching world God's power to transform lives. Yes, a call back to kindness would certainly be in order, not only for the women of Crete then, but also for our own young women today, who are growing up in this very context right now. Selfless, sacrificial service is not just noticeable in the context of a society given to laziness like Crete was. It is a beacon of light and beauty in a culture where everyone is consumed with his or her own personal agenda. Kindness, like all of the other behaviors and attributes targeted in Titus 2:3-5, is universally understandable, and those who are fluent in it will communicate God's love and power to transform lives effectively, unhindered by cultural and historical boundaries.

In summary, the word that Paul uses to describe what older women are to do with younger women appears to have been intentionally chosen because of the distinctive nuance that it carries. There were plenty of other words that Paul had access to that could have been used to describe "training" or "teaching," but this particular term, which was extremely rare in Paul's day, is the one that he chose. It carries with it the idea of "calling someone back to their senses."[31] This fit the context of what was needed in the church in Crete, and it fits the context of what is needed today.

PIVOTAL AND FOUNDATIONAL

Return with me now to the claim I began with: Realizing that Titus 2:4 is speaking about *calling young women to get back on track*, rather than simply training them, is pivotal to understanding the whole concept of mentoring as it is outlined in Titus 2.

This is because the meaning of *sophronizo* significantly impacts what mentors do with mentees. Some have proposed that mentoring is simply living decent lives so younger women can observe them, and

> *Calling back assumes correction, re-direction, and re-training are necessary.*

then just hoping for the best. [32] Magically, mystically, almost as if by some form of osmosis, the young women are expected to somehow catch on and "end up" doing the things they ought to do. This is clearly neither training nor calling back! Others propose that a teaching program will do the trick. A teaching approach is far better than the live-and-hope approach, but it still falls short of both training and "calling back" because a number of elements are still missing. Training is intentional to be sure, and it has life change as its goal. Like calling back, training is also proactive and personalized. But as we have now seen, *"calling back" has certain additional elements that go beyond training.* It assumes that correction, redirection, and retraining will be necessary.

Let's take a closer look at this. Teaching and training both begin with a clean slate or build on what someone already knows. However, when someone has strayed from the truth or wandered from the path, they are not starting with a clean slate. They cannot just be trained. We need to recognize that in a very real sense, they've *already* been trained … by the culture. What is necessary now, before any retraining in godliness can occur, is correction and cleansing. If you are a seamstress you may

---

[31] The NKJV translates the word *sophronizo* "admonish." I think they were on to something there!

[32] See, e.g., Connie Witt and Cathi Workman, *That Makes Two of Us* (Loveland, CO: Group, 2009).

liken this to the difference between
making something from a new piece of
cloth and completely altering every seam
of a previously made garment. The seam

*They've already been
trained…by the culture.*

ripping and altering of measurements, and reshaping, realigning, and
restitching are far more time consuming and difficult than cutting the
pieces and assembling them in the first place.

*As I anticipated our second son's wedding, I embarked on what became
quite a journey: the process of acquiring an appropriate outfit. The first step
was finding a few options online; the next was trying to find them in actual
stores to confirm a proper fit and availability before making my final decision.
Well, the first trip resulted in not a single dress to try on after visiting nine
stores! On my second trip, one store had a dress from my list, but it was four
sizes too large. Now I had a dilemma. If I ordered my size in from another of
their stores and it did not fit, my only recourse would be a store credit. And that
would amount to just wasting the money since I couldn't see myself needing
another formal dress from this store any time in the near future. The salesclerk
encouraged me instead to have their alteration specialist give me an estimate
for sizing the dress down. "Miss Alteration Lady" arrived quickly and began
measuring, quoting separate prices for each seam involved. Before she even got
through the bodice, the price was significantly higher than the cost of the entire
dress! And that particular outfit had an attached skirt which was tiered and
included a jacket as well. As one seeking to be a good steward, there was really
no point in taking any more measurements.*

Alterations are costly. Similarly, calling someone who is off track
back to her senses is going to be costly. In the case of mentoring, the
cost involved will depend to a large extent on how far off track she has
gotten, as well as on her willingness and motivation to get back on track.

Planting a tree in a freshly tilled garden is one task. Removing an
old established stump before the tilling can even begin in preparation
for planting the new sapling is quite another! I speak from experience.
In our case, the "correction" process eventually culminated with hiring
a tractor to pull out the remains of the stump after a variety of methods

had failed to remove it. Since the stump was located in our front yard, we provided quite a range of entertainment for our neighbors in the process! Sometimes it will take many attempts to help a younger woman see or accept where she has gone astray from God's values and standards and embraced the thinking of the world that permeates the air she has grown up breathing. Just as we experimented first with trying to slow-burn the stump of our weeping birch tree and then trying to dig it out, as mentors we may have to prayerfully approach our mentee's issues from many angles before we achieve the desired result.

So, calling back does not begin with a clean slate. It assumes that there will be significant issues that will have to be addressed and corrected. It is therefore far more involved than simply "beginning from scratch." A missionary friend of mine wrapping up a home assignment and preparing to return to the Muslim world penned the following lines to me: "Discipling in a Muslim country is like taking a child to the zoo. Discipling in N. America is like finding a guy with a skin rash, buried up to the neck in fine dry sand, and digging him out with a fork… [It is very] labor intensive because of such entrenched strongholds in the church. In the Muslim world there are so few to disciple. But here there are whole churches full of folk who may have been redeemed but have never been taught to obey all that Christ has commanded us… [It is] really labor intensive."

I thought, "Amazing!" How graphic and relevant for highlighting the difference between training and getting someone back on track. His words captured much of what makes the latter so much more involved than mere training. They speak of the pre-training work, the elements of complexity, dedication, patience, and tenderness that are required, and the oftentimes painstaking and lengthy nature of the task (digging sand with a fork!). And then, once the rescue has been accomplished, the training, really retraining, must begin. Calling back is indeed far more involved than simply training.

TRAINING, RETRAINING, AND THE NEED FOR REDIRECTION

Getting back on track speaks of redirecting. This involves training-like activities, but also much more. An overweight and out of shape boxer will need to redirect his eating and workout routine if he wants to reenter the ring with any hope of a successful fight. One who eats like a football player, but does not exercise like one will not end up fit, but fat. His lack of exercise signals a need for redirection. We would also likely agree that a cardiologist who has left off performing heart surgeries and is now heavily invested in redecorating various hospital wards—picking out new paint colors and carpet—has gotten off track. Just as the jogger who has slowed to a saunter or complete stop, exploring the flora and fauna along the path through the wooded park, is off track.

As an aspiring beach power-walker I understand this last example well. More often than I care to admit, my stride slows or even stops abruptly as my attention is riveted on the remains of another of God's amazing creations strewn on the beach. My loving husband then performs the crucial role of getting me back on track. This comes in many forms. "Don't look down! Eyes straight ahead!" spoken in mock sergeant tones. Or even, "I'm leaving you behind," tossed over his shoulder as he continues on briskly down the shoreline. Some days I prefer to stroll home with pockets full and a heart even more full of praise to God for the beauty of His world, power walk long since abandoned. But the fact is, it is not possible to work up a sweat, give my heart and lungs a workout, and tone my muscles if day after day I stroll, collect shells, and admire the sunrise. These are two different goals, two different tracks. Someone who is going the wrong way needs to be redirected.

INTENTIONAL AND PROACTIVE

One key point about recalling someone to get them back on track is that this endeavor is by nature both *intentional* and *proactive*. This precludes at least two other things. First, since the learning that takes place in mentoring is intentional, it will be neither incidental nor accidental. Both the remedial and the training elements of *sophronizo* will require that the mentor is proactive.

> *Getting someone back on track is by nature both intentional and proactive.*

She is not just aimlessly getting together and "hanging out with her mentee," enjoying her company with no thought for what is being taught or accomplished, with no plan or objectives or real purpose in mind. No. God has called older women to ensure younger women get on track and remain on track. This calling gives a mentor the authority to set the direction, to plot a course of action (following God's master curriculum), and even to make demands without apology.

"Really?" you ask, "I don't think I heard that right…make demands?" Yes. But before you throw in the towel, think with me about some other examples of training, from preparation for a marathon to preparation for an hour-long instrumental recital to military, or technical, or medical training. Demands and standards are always an indispensable part of training, as is discipline. Conductors do not apologize for rehearsals or recitals. Professors do not apologize for assignments designed to prepare their students to do life-saving surgeries. Sergeants do not apologize for awakening new recruits at the crack of dawn, not even when it appears to the new recruit that he has been awakened for meaningless activity! In truth, though, he was not. Always there is a plan, even if the only goal for the early rising is just to train him to obey his commanding officer without question. It is still preparation for the day when obedience to such a command may save his life. Likewise, in mentoring we have God-given goals. There is a purpose. There are standards. There is a curriculum, and there needs to be a plan. There may be many approaches available to us, many ways to accomplish the goals, but every mentor is to be moving her mentee in her own unique way towards the same goal, intentionally. And each mentor should follow God's master curriculum as she plots her course of action. The corrective aspect of *sophronizo* only adds weight to the intentionality necessary. Remember, typically we would expect it to take more initiative, planning, and effort to prepare an unhealthy, out of shape participant for a marathon than it would a fit athlete.

Secondly, because training is both *intentional* and *proactive*, it precludes adopting an approach in which various crises in the mentee's life are permitted to set the direction and tone for all that transpires when the two meet together. That would be a *reactive* approach. The existence of a curriculum implies that there will be at least some principle-driven time. We know that God has given us both goals to work towards and a curriculum to follow. These are found all throughout His Word, but they are summarized rather well in the Great Commission (Matt. 28:19-20). And as you are well aware by now, the specialized women's curriculum is found in Titus 2:4-5. We will return to the issue of what is actually done when mentor and mentee meet momentarily, as well as how to go about choosing specific content and goals on which to focus. For now, we have taken the initial step of recognizing that the meaning of *sophronizo* implies that mentoring will not be directed solely by the mentee's experiences, needs, crises, or wishes.

IMPLICATIONS FOR MENTOR QUALIFICATIONS
The meaning of *sophronizo* effectively reinforces the importance of maturity on the part of the mentor. She must know the standards that God calls women to live up to well. She herself must be well grounded. She must be on track.

Willingness to Do the Hard Things
We have seen that calling back involves a role that is not present in training; it addresses ways in which the mentee is straying or misguided in her thinking or actions. This implies that a mentor must be willing to address areas where a mentee is off track and correct her, calling her back to a life that glorifies God. This can be a difficult thing to do, but mentors must be willing to do the hard things.

As mentors, we know we are accountable to God. Fear of God both compels and empowers us to do the hard things. We know we will stand before the Sovereign God one day and give an account of how we obeyed Him in every area of our lives, including this one.

Excellent mentors will help their mentees see not just *that* they have strayed, but *why* they have strayed, so that they can avoid recurrences. This means they will partner in the process of helping their mentees *identify* where they have assimilated to the world. They will then *support* them in the process of escaping from assimilation, and embracing the renewal of their minds and the transformation of their lives (Rom. 12:1-2). This is not an easy task!

Greater Level of Active Involvement

Calling back, therefore, implies that the mentor will have a level of familiarity and active involvement with her mentee that allows her to see what is off track in her mentee's life. This will require a trusting, open relationship. It will require honesty on the part of both women, and mutual vulnerability. Perhaps most of all, it will require spending sufficient time together on a regular basis in order to allow the mentor to be able to identify where her mentee needs help. A lack of any of these elements can impede the mentor's ability to correctly determine where her mentee is off track.

Various factors can actually hinder rather than promote the development of familiarity and involvement that is needed. For example, a casual "on call" approach to mentoring where contact occurs solely at the initiative of the mentee does not provide for this. It allows a mentee to keep any errant ways hidden, and could severely inhibit the regular contact that is needed for a mentor to observe and accurately identify areas where her mentee needs help. Furthermore, a mentee who is aware that she is straying, but who is not yet able or willing to leave the temptation behind, is unlikely to initiate contact.

Factors that prohibit or inhibit the development of trust and vulnerability abound. However, keeping confidences; showing genuine love, acceptance, care, and interest; clearly demonstrating that you have her best interest and her maturity in Christ as your sole objectives; and setting an example of being open yourself can all go a long way to helping your mentee gain the level of comfort and trust with you that she needs to help her open up. If a mentor is to successfully *sophronizo* her mentee, honesty, a close relationship, and active involvement in her mentee's life will usually be necessary.

As I have tried to flesh out some of the nuances communicated by the word *sophronizo* for you, I hope you have been able to get a better grasp of the meaning it carries. As a final illustration, picture a rut in a dirt lane that the wheels of a cart keep falling back into. It is much easier to direct the cart down a new path than it is to take it down the old one with the ruts and stay clear of them. *Misunderstanding the meaning of* sophronizo *and substituting "training" for "calling back" could lead to missing these crucial elements of mentoring, and thereby sidestepping or undermining this very necessary and important part of the complete process.*

In the end, the message is this: As those who identify with Christ, we cannot be pulled by our culture in all sorts of other directions, "every which way," away from what God wants us to be. For this reason, God has directed that older women are taught to be godly so they can perform a crucial role, and that is to call younger women back to specific standards and behaviors that are clearly God-ordained and God-honoring. They are to issue a wake-up call. They are to get them back on track.

IMPLICATIONS FOR CURRICULUM: PERSONAL TRAINERS

We will explore how to get a younger woman back on track, and what mentees need to be trained to do in the chapters that follow on Approaches and Subjects to Broach. However, as I wrestled with how to balance allowing the mentee's life experiences and needs to direct the mentoring process with the explicit content and goals of mentoring that Scripture sets out, I realized that the two-pronged approach that this required could probably be described as a personal training program. It is a personal (re)training program designed by God, but specifically tailored for the particular mentee. The direction and content of the mentoring sessions must be driven by *both* what has been outlined by God in Scripture *and* the needs that are identified or perceived by both mentor and mentee. This fits perfectly with the remedial and training aspects of *sophronizo* that we have discussed, and highlights the need for biblical mentoring to be planned and intentional. Only then will we reach our goal of the mentee being transformed into a perfect Christ-follower who brings glory to God.

CONTENT SOURCES

Loosely speaking, the content for your mentoring sessions will come from three general sources. Some content will directly relate to your mentee's life experiences. Typically, such content surfaces naturally as you answer questions your mentee may ask or as you respond to a need she may share or a concern she may express. This content is thus driven by her specific needs and circumstances. Our assignment as mentors, however, is to get our mentees back on track so they will bring honor to God's name and the gospel; and the questions, needs, and experiences that they bring to our attention each week may or may not relate to this goal. The fact is, a mentee may or may not be able to even see for herself where she is off track. Quite often we are the last people to be able to see what everyone else around us has perceived about us for ages. We all tend to be blind to our own faults, and we are easily self-deceived and self-deluded. Remember Jesus' story about the log and the speck (Matt 7:3-5)? This human tendency to be blind to our own sins and shortcomings makes it all the more important that mentors not base the content of their interactions only on the felt needs of their mentees.

A second source is crucial: "God's curriculum," the content prescribed in Scripture. Although the issues raised in Scripture may not currently be on the mentee's radar at all, her mentor knows that she needs this training to grow to maturity in Christ. Here, the mentor is standing on God's promise that "All Scripture is God-breathed and is useful for teaching, rebuking, correction and training in righteousness, [17] so that the man of God [or woman of God] may be thoroughly equipped for every good work" (2 Tim. 3:16-17). Perfection, or maturity in Christ, will always require broad instruction in the whole counsel of God.

Finally, some of the mentoring "content" will come in the form of character development exercises and practical application. Again, this will be largely designed by the mentor as a direct outgrowth of both biblical commands and needs in the mentee, whether the needs are unique to her (a particular gifting or weakness) or simply common needs among believers. Or, perhaps the needs are relevant for a subset of believers of which the mentee is a part, such as single women, young married women, or women who have had a particular experience. For example, young women whose trust has been betrayed may all profit from similar exercises designed to help them trust people again, and even to actively renew or deepen their trust in God, rather than just accepting or acknowledging the truth that He is trustworthy. As a mentor, you can reference both biblical commands and your mentee's needs as you seek God's guidance in planning application and accountability exercises for her. This third category of "content" targets behavioral change. The behavioral changes that are worked into a mentee's life through these exercises, practical application, and accountability agreements will be closely related to the new truths learned and insights gained in the second category of content. In fact, changes seen will often actually be the fruit resulting from that instruction as well, since a change in thinking often precedes a change in behavior.

As another example, consider a single woman who is being taught to work with all her might for the Lord while she is unencumbered by the responsibilities of being a wife and mother. She may be asked to make a list of ways she has been able to invest her time in God's kingdom in the absence of other duties. She may be asked to prayerfully consider a wider scope of ministry or training. She may be challenged to intentionally pursue a focus of giving thanks to God for this increased opportunity, and keep a record of her successes and failures in giving thanks. You may need to begin by asking her to seek God to even have the desire to be thankful or to want to serve Him to the fullest of her ability. She may need to be encouraged to submit to God's will in this area of singleness, and be supported by you in the process of relinquishing the good, God-given desire to get married as she presents herself as a living sacrifice to Him. If getting married has become an idol, then exercises designed to address this sin would all fit under this form of practical "content" born out of and designed to support the related information content.

PLANNING, "PROBING," AND PRAYING

Planning what needs to be covered does not preclude speaking with a mentee, even at length, about a relevant issue in her life. I have found that the two can at times be quite compatible and work well together in training her. However, as we have seen, calling back and training are very different from and do not allow for a series of crises or whims in the mentee's life to be the sole factor that determines the direction, tone, or content of mentoring. There is so much biblical content to cover that mentors have no need for purposeless probing in a mentee's life. And certainly there is no license for this. Know, however, that sometimes the issues a mentee most needs your help with may be those that she is unable to recognize on her own as yet, and they may not be immediately visible to you either. You may need her help to bring them to the surface, and she may need you to help her to see them for what they are. Take the time to seek God's Holy Spirit to direct you. It will be time well invested. He will show you the specifics of how much to plan and how much to allow your mentee's life to guide your time together.

There is one more consideration you may want to tuck away for future reference. There are certain times when people are more receptive to learning than other times. These heightened moments of teachability quite often occur when a person is faced with a crisis or a particularly challenging issue. As mentors, if we are aware of this we can make the most of these opportunities to encourage, teach, train, and shepherd. Sometimes we will have no advance warning of a particularly teachable moment. In these times, our own walk with the Lord and our vital, fresh, abiding relationship with Him is our lifeline and best resource. Always pray for guidance in the moment. Be humble, vulnerable, and candid as well. Admit when you are not prepared to deal with an issue that presents itself without prior warning and with which you have had no experience or feel out of your comfort zone.

Other times we will have some advance notice, or perhaps an issue may be ongoing for a more extended period of time. Perhaps it will involve a recurring theme in your mentee's life. In such cases, take advantage of the opportunity for specific preparation ahead of time. This includes bathing your mentee and the circumstances in prayer, and studying what God's Word has to say about a situation or what principles it includes that are relevant to it. But remember also that God's powerful Holy Spirit indwells you and empowers you as you remain a clean vessel at His disposal. If you are clean from the common and mundane in your thinking and life you can be useful to Him for the noble purposes (2 Tim. 2:20-21). If you are submitting to Him, He will fill you and use you to help guide, exhort, advise, comfort, challenge, and train your mentee in godliness.

Let's close with a concrete example. Young women are commanded by God to be pure. At the same time, our society puts an incredible amount of pressure on young women today to be impure. A wise mentor will address with her mentee the specifics of what obedience to

God and resisting the culture's pressure in this area looks like. They may discuss purity of thoughts, of dress, and of actions. In light of the goal of purity, a wise mentor may ask her mentee, "What should a Christian woman allow into her mind through her eyes, and what should she not? What will develop an appetite for purity and modesty in a woman, and what will tempt her away from God's norms and towards the world's?" A wise mentor will guide her mentee to see the folly of inching as close to the world's values and standards as possible without actually crossing an arbitrary or self-determined line. She will lead her mentee to set the course of her life in the right direction.

CASE IN POINT

One case from my own experience beautifully illustrates an instance where a mentee's question dovetailed perfectly with "required curriculum" content. Jess was an elegant and sweet spirited college student who was heading off to counsel at a camp. She asked if she could bring a new bathing suit over to my home and try it on for me. She wanted my opinion. She wanted reassurance that she would be dressed acceptably ...not in terms of fashion, but in a manner that would not cause any of the males present to stumble. She was a wise girl! Men in their 70s still struggle with lust. And young pubescent boys do as well. Jess also recognized that although her primary responsibility was towards her younger female campers, her sphere of influence included fellow female counselors too, and she did not want to be a poor example to any of the females present either. In the end, we both ended up trying on suits together, all the while learning and growing and sharing. I still fondly recall that evening spent engaged in rich conversation and sharing of our lives, all in an effort to move towards greater obedience to God in the area of purity. Modesty is part of God's curriculum ("to be pure," Titus 2:5), and it was relevant to Jess' current life issues as well.

LESSON PLANS

The concept of recalling someone to their senses or getting them back on track provides a perfect framework for developing a lesson plan for mentoring. If you are calling your mentee back to a standard, you have the absolute nonnegotiable standard on the one side, and your mentee's individual position relative to that standard on the other. Some of what you do in your time with her will be determined by her life and issues, and some by the set standards God has established for us. The set of prescribed topics God has provided will be your anchor. These are the areas on which we will focus our particular attention as we seek to pull our younger women back on course. The storm waves will come at our mentees from every direction. *Our God-given assignment is to hold them on course—steady, grounded, stable, clinging to the anchor regardless of the force of the storm or the size of the waves. When they are knocked off course, it is our task to get them back on track; when they wander off, we are to call them back.*

Chapter 5

APPROACHES TO MENTORING
AND SOME SPECIAL
CONSIDERATIONS

Now it's time to get down to the nitty gritty, the nuts and bolts of mentoring. *How* do we get younger women back on track? "Just live and let the younger women see you," say some, "and 'they will end up as models of goodness.'"[33] I don't see this happening. It's *not* happening. This "approach" has an almost magical air to it. It assumes many things. One can almost hear the poof of the fairy's wand as the younger woman "ends up a model of goodness."

When we truly understand the task of getting a younger woman back on track, however, it can seem huge and overwhelming. Where do we begin? What will our method be? Advice for mentoring approaches abound.

---

[33] See the paraphrase of Titus 2:1-6 in *The Message*.

Let's accommodate what the younger women want, meet on their terms, not be "the Bible answer woman," and not make demands or require a regular time commitment.[34]

Let's pacify their consciences…revel in receiving their appreciation…and call it "mentoring in the moment."[35]

Let's pamper them with gourmet meals, help them improve their cooking skills, and boost their confidence for entertaining. Add to this some good biblical teaching on six topics…and call it a wrap. (No pun intended.) We'll get it all done in seven weeks.[36]

Still others propose helping "young friends" with a wide range of personal goals and desires…that are far more closely aligned with worldly or cultural values than with God's expressed will.[37]

Sometimes the advice is short, sweet, and appealing, insomuch as it apparently lightens the load for the mentor:

Be a friend.
Offer a listening ear.
Encourage.
Go for coffee.
Watch movies together.[38]
And remember the cardinal rule: "Do not criticize their technology!"[39]

---

[34] Sue Edwards and Barbara Neumann, *Organic Mentoring* (Grand Rapids, MI: Kregel Ministry, 2014).

[35] Witt and Workman, *That Makes Two of Us*, 50–52.

[36] Betty Huizenga, *Apples of Gold: A Six-Week Nurturing Program for Women* (Colorado Springs, CO: David C. Cook, 2000), 10–11.

[37] Van Atta, *Women Encouraging Women*, 63; Witt and Workman, *That Makes Two of Us*, 92–93.

[38] Fryling, *Disciplemakers' Handbook*, 96; Witt and Workman, *That Makes Two of Us*, 92.

[39] Edwards and Neumann, *Organic Mentoring*, 151.

All of these have been proposed or endorsed as methods, activities, or approaches for mentoring. If the goal is truly getting younger women back on track, however, these means will not accomplish it. Perhaps you have encountered similar ideas, but now realize that the biblical foundation laid in the first few chapters precludes many of these suggestions. God's Word is our standard. It is our foundation. It is the authority for all that we do. This was the anchor that held me in place when the storm waves threatened. Without a tight grip on it, I too would have been swept off course. Yes. It's confession time again.

A SECOND FALSE START!

I'm taking you on this journey with me. As a fellow human, my own experience just adds weight to the message and warning I am seeking to impress on you. It serves to show how very easy it is to get off track. So here we go. I originally began this section with the following words.

> Let's begin by acknowledging that this is where we leave off direct scriptural injunction and venture into human wisdom. God has allowed much variety in His world and among people, and He uses much creativity and variation in dealing with each of us! He has given each of us different gifts for the mutual building up of the whole family of God. He promises to guide us as we look to Him for guidance, with the pure motives of bringing Him glory and advancing His kingdom. He has promised, He is able, and He will do it—He will build His church and present a perfect, spotless, beautiful bride to His Son, all in good time. Let's allow Him to show each of us where we fit in.

Most of this is actually true. So why would I revise it in the first place, and even more so, why would I consider it valuable to openly share this with you? My hope is that this will bring home to you the importance of knowing God's Word well, holding to it tenaciously, and not being moved off course by our culture. You see, although everything else remains true, the very first statement is not. It was based on a false assumption, and again, making a false assumption was leading me astray. Saying we had reached the stage where we needed to leave Scripture and begin to plumb the depths of human wisdom had actually seemed reasonable to me. After all, this was the unmistakable pattern in the plethora of material I had read on mentoring. With few exceptions, the vast array of ideas that

There is no reason to set Scripture aside when it does actually speak to this, too.

were suggested, promoted, or authoritatively prescribed all indicated that at this stage of the game we were pretty much on our own. The message ranged from "Here are my suggestions," to "This is what you will need to do to succeed." The idea was either something along the lines of "use the mind God gave you and figure it out" or "this is what worked for me; go thou and do likewise."

Before following where others had led, though, I needed to ask a very basic question. *Does* Scripture speak to this issue? When I explored the answer, I found that indeed it did. There is no reason to set Scripture aside when it does actually have what we need. Remember, "All Scripture is God-breathed and is useful for teaching, rebuking, correcting and training in righteousness, so that the man of God may be *thoroughly equipped for every good work*" (2 Tim. 3:16-17, emphasis added). We *can* continue to base everything on Scripture. How easily I could have veered off course! How serious the repercussions could have been!

As we delve into the amazing resource God has given us in Scripture, we find the following examples of methods and approaches being used to accomplish the goals of mentoring: teaching, modeling, serving together, and many of the components of what I call eclectic sessions. We see mentoring happening in groups, one-on-one, and "two-on-one." We even find long-distance mentoring in Scripture! What we do *not* find mentioned in its pages is the ubiquitous book study of today.

TWO MAIN APPROACHES: MODELING AND SESSIONS

Two of the main ways we observe mentoring taking place in Scripture are through the use of a modeling approach or a session approach. While teaching and serving together are important activities recorded in

Scripture repeatedly, these seem more fittingly viewed as components of the other approaches than as fully developed approaches on their own. Similarly, long-distance mentoring will not be treated as its own full-fledged approach, but rather as an adaptation of another approach.

Jesus utilized both session and modeling approaches at various times, and eventually you may want to use some combination of both yourself. Basically, in modeling, your mentee is invited to learn through observation, conversation, and participating in life experiences with you; and in sessions, mentor and mentee spend concentrated time sharing together verbally. These largely verbal exchanges cover a wide range of distinct types of conversations and activities, making the session approach very eclectic in nature.

The next few chapters will explore the subject of approaches to mentoring in greater depth. These introductory pages offer a brief overview of teaching and serving together as two components that can be incorporated into either a session or a modeling approach. We will then take a closer look at modeling as an approach in Chapter 6, examining its biblical basis and its components. In Chapter 7 we will explore the session approach along with its biblical basis and components. Finally, in Chapter 8, we will consider some of the issues germane to the subject of book studies. We will conclude the section on approaches with a comparison of the two approaches. Long-distance mentoring and group mentoring will be briefly addressed in Appendices.

TEACHING

Teaching is a comprehensive, wide-ranging activity. It encompasses many areas. For our purposes of mentoring, we will consider the areas of content-focused teaching, teaching specific life skills, and teaching spiritual disciplines.

Content-Focused Teaching

Most content-focused teaching will generally fall under one of three categories. The first is Bible Studies, where a book of the Bible is taught. All Scripture is given to us to help us grow in the knowledge of God and become conformed to the likeness of His Son. These goals are the goals of mentoring. Teaching your mentee any book of the Bible would be a valuable component of mentoring.

Another sub-category of content-focused teaching would be topical studies. In a topical study, the goal is to explore and uncover what the Bible has to say about a particular subject. The potential for topical studies is vast, as the Bible covers such a wide array of subjects. We must be particularly cautious, though, to handle God's Word correctly when preparing a topical study. Beginning with preconceived biases, particularly those born of or strongly influenced by the world's thinking, is a recipe for trouble. Whenever we talk about teaching, it is appropriate to sound a warning. The more fully we understand the fear of God, the more we will welcome the reminder. If we truly fear God, we will take to heart the words of James 3:1 ("Not many of you should presume to be teachers, my brothers, because you know that we who teach will be judged more strictly"). As we explore what Scripture has to say about a given issue, it is critical that each verse referenced is correctly interpreted in its context. This means more than just reading a few verses before or after it. It means more than reading a chapter or two that surrounds it. There are many considerations that need to be taken into account. There are many types of context. Literary context, historical context, and a host of other factors all provide clues that enable us to eliminate what a verse could not possibly be saying, and to understand the intended message of each verse more clearly and accurately. *How to Read the Bible for All Its Worth* is one resource that offers assistance for anyone who would benefit from some more guidance or instruction in the area of biblical interpretation.[40]

Finally there is the content that is addressed as various doctrines of the faith are taught. This content focuses on what the Bible has to say about the different doctrines. This is one type of topical study; the same cautions we discussed above apply.

In all of this, our best resource is the Bible itself. It is our foundation and guide. It is our standard and the authority for what we teach and what we do. I am in good company when I recommend keeping your

---

[40] Douglas Stuart and Gordon Fee, *How to Read the Bible for All Its Worth* (Grand Rapids, MI: Zondervan, 2003).

primary focus on the Bible. Through the ages one commendable "pillar of the faith" after another has come to this same conclusion. George Müller, who wrote the book on living by faith, both figuratively and literally, shares how he began his life with a library of books and ended with the one Book he found most valuable.[41] Likewise, famous cricketer turned missionary and founder of WEC (Worldwide Evangelisation for Christ), C. T. Studd, by the end of his life had reduced the books he considered worth his time right down to one.[42] Most important, Scripture itself claims to be a book unlike any other.[43] The supremacy of Scripture should be recognized first. This being established firmly in our minds, we can then consider some of the other resources that could be useful in the study of God's Word.

Not all resources should be weighed equally. I personally place concordances in a category by themselves as an invaluable tool. An exhaustive concordance will allow you to see at a glance every place where a specific word occurs in Scripture. This is an indispensable tool when you want to quickly find a verse you are looking for. How many times do we know a verse or an idea is in the

Not all resources should be weighed equally.

Bible, but find ourselves unable to remember the reference? If, like me, you have found yourself trying to locate a verse by flipping through the pages of your Bible, looking at the upper right hand side of each page where you think you last saw it, then it is time to make a closer acquaintance with this resource.

A concordance can also be helpful for studying a topic, or gaining a more rounded picture of a particular concept. You can readily look up different forms of the same word, which will be located nearby in the concordance, as words are listed in alphabetical order. This means that when you look up "pierce" for example, you will also readily see

---

[41] George Muller, *The Autobiography of George Muller* (New Kensington, PA: Whitaker House, 1985), 9, 31.
[42] Norman Grubb, *C. T. Studd, Cricketer and Pioneer* (London: Lutterworth Press, 1995), 218–219.
[43] See 2 Timothy 3:15-16; 2 Peter 1:20-21; Psalm 19:7; Isaiah 55:11; Matthew 24:35; John 6:63; Romans 10:17.

"pierced", "pierces", and "piercing". Many years ago now, I traded in my old *Strong's Concordance* for an electronic one that was available through my *BibleWorks* program. An online concordance (word search) such as those available through Bible Gateway or Blue Letter Bible provides easier and more convenient access than a large tome, especially when it is needed while traveling.

We access words in our concordances using the English gloss, which is the English word into which the Greek has been translated. The version of the Bible that is used and the quality of the translation are factors that influence the effectiveness of your concordance use. My old Strong's was linked solely to the King James Version; *BibleWorks* allows me to find the words used in any of 150 versions in many languages. You can do the same thing through biblegateway.com without purchasing a program.

Then there are resources that are helpful, but need to be used with caution, such as dictionaries and commentaries. Dictionaries, in particular, can easily lead us astray. They can be helpful if we encounter a theological term such as "sanctification" or "propitiation." However, looking up a word that you are already familiar with will typically lead you to read something into the passage that is not there. This stems from the fact that the English word you are looking up will only overlap in meaning with the Greek word it translates at one specific point. It will not have the same *range* of meanings as the Greek term, nor carry the same range of nuances. So, using a dictionary can lead to thinking that certain meanings or nuances associated with the English term were part of what the biblical writer was communicating, when in fact they would have never crossed the mind of either the author or original readers of the passage.

Like dictionaries, the use of commentaries and other books written by fellow believers also requires a measure of caution. They often share valuable and helpful insights. In reading them we can benefit from the years of study that their authors have invested in order to come to their level of understanding or expertise. Sometimes, however, these resources reflect the thinking of the world instead of God's truth, or include poor scholarship or misinterpretation, and we need to be mindful of this.

This brings us full circle, effectively reminding us that as we ourselves teach content, we too must be careful to exercise caution in our own teaching. In our role as teachers, we too will be judged more strictly. We must therefore remind ourselves again of the two incomparable resources that have been made available to us: the living Word of God and God Himself as our Teacher. We must purpose to lean heavily on the Holy Spirit, who leads us into all truth, to help us to accurately handle and teach His Word.

Specific Life Skills

A second sphere of teaching is the teaching of life skills. God calls younger women to be "working at home" (ESV) or "busy at home" (NIV) in Titus 2:5; and in order to do this, they need to acquire the necessary skills. Thus, one part of the biblical basis for teaching life skills to our younger women is found in the call for younger women to run their households well. Another part is found in Titus 2:4, which identifies the relationships between husband and wife and mother and child as critically important ones to work on. The home is the primary sphere where these relationships are nurtured, and again, many life skills are necessary for the home to function smoothly. Finally, Titus 2:5 also focuses on character traits like self-control. Lack of self-control or clear thinking has caused the financial ruin of many homes and marriages. Thus, Titus 2 offers a biblical basis for teaching budgeting skills as well as character development, since each of these clearly contribute to living in one's home and managing one's household in such a way that God's honor is upheld and His reputation guarded.

Clearly, when Titus 2:5 calls for younger women to be busy at home, overseeing the affairs of their homes well, it assumes the ability to execute many tasks competently. Looking at the description of the imaginary model wife found in Proverbs 31 and other passages that speak of exemplary women, like Acts 9:36, 39 and 1 Timothy 5:4-14, helps to round out a picture for us of just how far-ranging and diverse these tasks and the related life skills can be. It is true that some of the specifics will be different for homemakers today, but many remain the same, and certainly the focus on the well-being of one's family and home has not changed.

Life skills may be divided into those that improve the way the home is run and those that facilitate better relationships. Teaching home-oriented life skills can involve both practical, hands-on experience and verbal instruction or "book learning." This sort of "home improvement" is not limited to maintenance, repairs, or renovations! Many skills can facilitate running a home well:

- meal preparation
- how to handle common illnesses of adults, children, and infants
- how to respond to certain emergencies
- the mechanics of cleaning, home organization, laundry, and ironing
- managing bills and budgeting
- sewing, mending, needlework, knitting, crocheting
- caring for guests
- using the gifts of entertainment and hospitality to further God's kingdom
- and, yes, even those skills needed to perform specific home repair, maintenance, or improvement projects

Some life skills that could facilitate better relationships include communication skills, listening skills, etiquette, child training, and self-discipline.

Spiritual Disciplines
The third sphere of teaching would be the teaching of spiritual disciplines. Prayer, Scripture meditation, and personal Bible reading are some of the most common and essential ones. Less commonly viewed as a spiritual discipline, but equally important, would be evangelism. Obedience and acts of service could also be viewed as spiritual

Life is short. How we invest our time and energies now will matter for eternity after.

disciplines. Some form of journaling, accountability, or self-evaluation could be another valuable spiritual discipline to consider.

There are some other activities that have grown out of ancient practices, but have no solid foundation in God's Word, which are sometimes regarded as spiritual disciplines.[44] I personally choose to avoid these and focus instead on what Scripture clearly commands. Life is short. How we invest our time and energies now will matter for eternity. Therefore, we must be wise and selective.

Even this brief perusal of just these three areas of teaching makes it clear that teaching is a wide-ranging activity. Nevertheless, it is not a complete approach to mentoring. Like serving together, it is an activity that can function as a component of either of the two main approaches.

SERVING TOGETHER

Serving together is another stand-alone component that can be incorporated into either a session or a modeling approach. As with teaching, examples of God's people serving together abound in Scripture. And many examples clearly involve a younger, less knowledgeable or less experienced servant of God serving alongside an older, more mature follower, who is setting an example and offering guidance. Again, Moses and Joshua, and Elijah and Elisha come readily to mind. In the New Testament we observe Barnabas taking John Mark under his wing (Acts 15:37-39), even as Paul does the same with Timothy (Acts 16:1-3). Perhaps the most detailed accounts, though, are found in the life of Jesus Himself. We can readily model this component of our mentoring after His example.

It may be stating the obvious, but a first step in serving together is that we must be serving to begin with. Jesus ministered to others. We must likewise be involved in serving others. And as we serve, we should actively seek to make our ministry a model for others to see and follow, just as Jesus did. Jesus told us to let our lights shine. Because our hearts are prone to deception, though, we must take care. We dare not serve to be recognized, thanked, or praised for our service, but neither should we hide our service out of a false humility or a desire to guard our area of service for ourselves. There is no place for territorialism in

---

[44] Prayer labyrinths, silence, prayer circles, and *lectio divina* are some examples.

God's kingdom. Still the fact remains that we cannot model if no one is aware of what we are doing. We cannot train others if we are doing our service in secret. Invite others to see you serving. After they have observed for a time, we should invite them to serve alongside us, just as Jesus did.[45] This allows us the opportunity to observe them in action, to offer guidance, correction, instruction, and encouragement. It allows for feedback and for practice. It enables a mentee to gain experience under supervision.

Jesus also sent His disciples out to minister on their own. The time will come when every mentor must do this as well. Depending on the area of service and the level of maturity in the mentee, this may happen very quickly, or a mentee may require an extended amount of joint ministry time before being ready to serve independently. This cannot be predicted.

Jesus debriefed His disciples after independent ministry, and He prepared them ahead of time. When we serve together with our mentees, we should offer them all that is necessary to help them succeed, to the best of our abilities. The active joint ministry experience itself, coupled with the instruction received during it, and any additional specific final instructions you give prior to independent ministry are all a part of guiding a mentee through the process of ministering together. Debriefing the experience with her afterwards is another important and beneficial part of the process.

How does this fit in with the unique call to get younger women back on track? What makes *this* serving together different than any other form of merely serving together? Many younger women today are not involved in any form of genuine active service intended to accomplish the job Jesus left us to do. Some have been steered off track by being led to believe they are serving others when they engage in activities primarily focused on meeting their own desires to be pampered. Serving involves meeting real needs. I truly understand the need for and value of rest, relaxation, and social interactions. However, when women are

Serving involves meeting real needs.

---

[45] Mark 6:35-44; 8:1-9.

led to believe that watching movies together, cooking gourmet meals for one another, planning pedicures, spa trips, or shopping trips are forms of serving one another, it could be an indication that they have been led off course. The God who calls us through His Son to deny ourselves (Matt. 16:24) is not a God of double standards. We may be deceived (Gal. 6:7), but He cannot be. He sees our actions clearly for what they are, and He readily discerns the motives of our hearts (Prov. 16:2; 1 Cor. 4:5). He understands our need for rest (Psalm 103:14; Mark 6:31; Matt. 11:29-30) and for fellowship (Psalm 68:6a), but He is not confused about what these mean or about how these are accomplished, as we sometimes seem to be. And He is not in the habit of making exceptions to His clear commands.

If women have been led to believe that planning activities that promote self-indulgence is an act of service, then rather than prolong the confusion and the disobedience that sometimes accompanies this thinking, it falls to godly older women to first talk sense into those who have been led astray in this way, and then to live out the truth of what we are actually called to do. Talking sense would mean correctly identifying activities that qualify as genuine service, and distinguishing them from those that do not. For example, there may be some things that are appropriate as part of a Christian's vacation or personal recreation plans, but which have no relation to acts of service.

Living out the truth of what we are actually called to do would involve participating together in genuine service, engaging in activities that clearly work towards fulfilling the mandate Jesus left His followers. When every person on earth is a believer and fully conformed to the image of Jesus, when there are no longer any hurts or needs, no more loneliness, broken relationships, or discouragement, no abuse, no abandoned children, no hunger, no sickness, no lack of clothing or housing, no weakness or pain, and no one who is overwhelmed with the cares or burdens of life, then and only then will there be no need for acts of genuine Christian service.

Using the process of serving together as a component of a mentoring approach can be summarized in this way:

- Let your mentee observe you in active ministry.
- Allow her to minister alongside you.
- Support her as she ministers independently of you, providing feedback and encouragement.
- And always follow John the Baptist's example: Rejoice when you are surpassed!

It was a glorious sunny day. Liz and I opted to combine our talking with a walk down to the river. Liz was not an official mentee. We had only met a few times, as I was able to find a bit of free time. However, though we hadn't made a formal commitment, our times and conversations together were very intentional right from the beginning. The day we first met each other I had told her she would be easy to love, and I had been right! Liz was also very teachable, and there had already been good accountability. Up to this point, our time together had consisted of her bringing a painting over, and us talking as we each worked on our own canvas.

Among the things we talked about were ministry, serving, and reaching out to the lost. Liz had lots of contact with believers, but far less with those who do not follow Jesus. As I encouraged her to explore a ministry that would involve her in the lives of the lost, I shared about how God orchestrated my meeting Annabel, a woman in her mid-seventies, at a time when she was keenly aware that she was about to become a widow. As we walked that day, I pointed out to Liz both where I had met Annabel and where she lived.

On a subsequent visit, I learned Liz had been taking steps to develop relationships with unbelievers for the ultimate purpose of sharing the gospel. Encouraged, I shared how God had continued my connection with Annabel, and how He had strengthened me for the task of sharing His love with her and her husband practically and through words at a time when my own strength had been depleted. I relayed how following this her husband had indeed died and how God directed me to visit her on the day of the burial, purely in obedience to His prompting, as I had had no knowledge of his death. I shared how two weeks later I had hosted a small luncheon for Annabel to introduce her to some other believers who shared common life experiences with her. Here again God enabled me and orchestrated the details, prompting another godly woman to graciously provide the meal.

On the occasion I want to tell you about now, the time I had available to meet with Liz was not convenient for her. She regretfully wrote to say so, but her email did not go through. God used this to confirm for her what she had been sensing: God was telling her to clear a bit of time in her schedule to see me. I had just learned that Liz was not only a visual artist, but also a vocal one, so when she confirmed she could come, I proposed we could walk, visit, or sing together if she liked. Then during the night, God gave me an idea, and I waited to see if she would bring her guitar. She did. After we had sung for a while, I asked what she thought about going over to sing for Annabel to cheer her up a bit. Time was limited, but we prayed, we went, and we found Annabel at home. We sang, we shared briefly, and we then debriefed in the car afterward, ending this session together with some time in prayer.

God has given Liz some amazing opportunities and open doors to speak about Him to others since then. And He has been empowering her to take them, and leave the results to Him, just as He has done with me. Talking about serving is a very important part of mentoring; participating in serving together is another.

Chapter 6

A MODELING
APPROACH

*Whatever you have learned or received or heard from me,
or seen in me— put it into practice.
And the God of peace will be with you. (Phil. 4:9)*

*Our gospel came to you not simply with words, but also with power,
with the Holy Spirit and with deep conviction. You know how we
lived among you for your sake. You became imitators of us and of
the Lord; in spite of severe suffering, you welcomed the message with
the joy given by the Holy Spirit. And so you became a model to all
the believers in Macedonia and Achaia. (1 Thess. 1:5-7)*

BIBLICAL BASIS

There is so much in these verses! We see both passages showcasing
how modeling is done using a combination of elements. There is

what is seen and what is taught. There are the words, the power of God, the Holy Spirit's presence, and conviction, along with the exemplary lives of Paul, Silas, and Timothy. We see how embracing the message and following the example resulted in those who followed becoming models themselves. Reproduction is taking place, the kingdom of God is spreading, godliness is being multiplied. In the same way, as godly older women live out the power of the gospel to transform lives, they will be examples worth following. As their mentees follow them, they too will become models that others can follow.

In the modeling approach, the mentor invites the mentee into her life and home and much learning takes place through observation and participation in the regular activities of life. While learning this way can be very effective and produce lasting results, there is nevertheless a limit to what can be learned by direct observation alone. For this reason, just as was the case with Paul and his co-authors, a variety of types of conversations also need to occur. Discussions of issues, time for asking and answering questions, and thinking through worldview and philosophical issues that relate to what is being modeled, such as working out what loving one's husband really looks like, and some of the reasons we are told to do this, will need to take place as well. Calling women back to the biblical standard and getting them back on track necessitates identifying where they have gotten off track, how they got off track, and how they can get back on track. Showing what being on track looks like is definitely an important part of the process, but it is only a part. Modeling and observation will be complemented by intentional teaching of skills and of biblical truths. For this reason, time needs to be set aside to talk through things in the modeling approach as well, and the teaching and learning of specific skills should also be planned, rather than left to chance. Conversations could include ideas from the ten points in Chapter 7 as appropriate, and accountability and prayer should definitely be included. We must, in fact, be just as intentional in this approach as we would be in a session approach. We must prepare for each of our mentoring times with prayer. We must plan ahead.

MODELING MUST BE INTENTIONAL

Modeling is teaching by example. It is not, however, the "live and hope" approach implied by *The Message*'s translation of Titus 2:2-5.[46] Teaching, training, and the calling back signified by the word *sophronizo* do not refer to activities that happen by chance. A modeling approach will therefore require *intentional* modeling and *intentional*

"Follow" signifies intentional action.

imitating. In 1 Corinthians 11:1, we read, "Follow my example, as I follow the example of Christ." "Follow" signifies intentional action. First Corinthians 11:1 could be a theme verse for the mentor who chooses to use a modeling approach. It is as she herself follows Christ that she is able to invite others to imitate her.

This verse also, however, has implications for the mentee. She too must be intentional and actively involved. Take a look at Philippians 3:17, particularly the second part. This verse could be a good guide for mentees in a modeling approach. First of all, it is directed at the followers. They are told to follow a good example: "Join with others in following my example, brothers. Take note of those who live according to the pattern we gave you." We see from the word "pattern" that a set of standards and behavior exists. And it is expected that these standards will be known by believers and familiar to them. Believers, including both mentors and mentees, need to know the pattern so that they will be able to assess who is living according to it. Knowing what to look for and what is to be imitated also requires a measure of discernment. It will do no good to follow a poor example! This verse tells us that those who live according to the pattern will be recognizable; their adherence to the standard will be visible. Therefore, intentionality on the part of the mentee will require a commitment to observe carefully, exercise discernment, and choose to intentionally imitate what is good.

---

[46] "Guide older women into lives of reverence so they end up as neither gossips nor drunks, but models of goodness. By looking at them, the younger women will know how to love their husbands and children, be virtuous and pure, keep a good house, be good wives. We don't want anyone looking down on God's Message because of their behavior."

Ultimately we are each responsible for our own actions. A mentor who leads a mentee astray will be responsible for doing so, but a mentee who chooses to follow a foolish or ungodly mentor is also responsible for her choice. First Corinthians 15:33 is a clear command for everyone: "Do not be misled: 'Bad company corrupts good character.'" And the warning, "He who walks with the wise grows wise, but a companion of fools suffers harm" (Prov. 13:20) should motivate mentees to consider carefully whom they will choose to imitate. Similarly, the striking warnings of Scripture place a great deal of responsibility on the mentor: "And if anyone causes one of these little ones who believe in me to sin, it would be better for him to be thrown into the sea with a large millstone tied around his neck" (Mark 9:42).

MODELING REQUIRES PLANNING

We have already established that *sophronizo* does not refer to an activity that happens by chance. If modeling is to be an effective method of mentoring, it must be done intentionally. Certainly, much can be learned simply by intentionally observing a godly woman as she goes about living her life in devotion to God. However, there will be many areas where more intentionality is needed on the part of the mentor. For these areas, a mentor will need to plan what will be modeled. This need for planning is something that, at least initially, may not be readily apparent. It can often be the case, though, that a modeling approach requires just as much planning as a more session-focused approach, possibly even more.

Accountability will be another necessary part of a modeling approach, and this too will require planning.

"No, you won't need to turn in weekly lesson plans."

Having just moved down to teaching Pre-Kindergarten in a public school, it took me a second to process the casual remark from my principal. Thankfully, my brain rallied. I remembered that the prevalent thinking of the day was that at the tender age of three or four it was more beneficial to plan for just one day at a time. Each day's plan would be formulated only after the previous day was over. This allowed teachers to take into account daily progress and to incorporate the results of daily evaluations into the next day's plans.

In some sense, planning mentoring activities is similar. It is very individualized and it is very dependent on the mentee's current stage of development. It builds on her most recent progress. Having said that, a number of suitable and necessary accountability activities can still be planned ahead and included on a master list; they can then be selected meeting by meeting as appropriate. Occasionally, a new one can also be developed or improvised on the spot to meet the need of the moment.

Finally, we have seen that supplemental instruction and conversations are also required with modeling, and these too will require planning. Even Jesus complemented his modeling in this way. He clearly exhibited the fruit of the Spirit, and He fleshed out for us how to practice a host of godly behaviors that run contrary to our sinful human natures, but he also enhanced the effectiveness of these living demonstrations by sermons that similarly challenged the current cultural thinking and our natural human inclinations. He actively taught the multitudes to live in the ways that they observed Him living before them. He asked penetrating questions and told thought provoking stories to drive the truths He wanted to teach deep into His listeners' hearts. With His own mentees, the twelve disciples, he modeled ministry, but He also then gave them instructions before sending them out to do likewise; and He debriefed their ministry trip with them upon their return. There is no reason to believe that these things happened by chance. Effective modeling is intentional and requires planning. It combines the two elements of teaching (or conversations) and modeling. It also has two prerequisites.

MODELING REQUIRES BIBLICAL LITERACY AND EXEMPLARY LIVING

The two prerequisites for modeling are knowing the standard and living an exemplary life. So far as knowing the standard goes, we have already stressed the importance of biblical literacy. It cannot be overstated. All mentors should always be doing their best to be familiar with the whole counsel of God's Word. We should all be daily immersed in it and renewed by it. This may be especially important for those who plan to mentor largely by means of modeling. The truths have to be internalized and lived out. Living an exemplary life has also been explored at length.

Some key areas in which we should be able to model godly womanhood are prayer, day to day life, Christian service, and evangelism. Of course, many others could be added to this list.

For example, as we encounter the inevitable challenges and trials of this life, we mentors are to model responses that are worthy of our calling as God's daughters. We model letting the peace of Christ rule in our hearts. We model the joy that is not dependent on circumstances. We model forgiveness and lack of bitterness and vengefulness. As we do so, we will not only be impacting our mentees and others for good, we will be bringing delight to our Father's heart and glory to His name. Mentors model strength of character, godly submission, mothering, and homemaking. As much as each one is able to in her own particular circumstances, let us showcase God's design for a healthy, fulfilling marriage. Model, encourage, and point your mentee to Jesus.

MODELING IS AN INDIVIDUALIZED ASSIGNMENT

In all of this, as you are seeking to be a role model, remember that there is only one of you…ever. Focus on God and His plan for you. Follow His leading. Seek to be free of peer, societal, or traditional pressure. Work to be free of others' expectations. Even our own expectations and goals can trip us up. We should be cognizant of this, even as we also acknowledge our own limitations.

God made you as He wished you to be and put you where He wants you. God is sovereign—so we should be content.[47] Each of us is to be an example, and each of us is also to be content and avoid comparisons.[48]

---

[47] "For you created my inmost being; you knit me together in my mother's womb. I praise you because I am fearfully and wonderfully made; your works are wonderful, I know that full well. My frame was not hidden from you when I was made in the secret place. When I was woven together in the depths of the earth, your eyes saw my unformed body. All the days ordained for me were written in your book before one of them came to be" (Psalm 139:13-16). See also Acts 17:26 and Philippians 4:11-12.

[48] Donna Otto has some good ideas for dealing with the trap of comparing one's self to others, and appreciating the actual person that God has made you to be. See *Finding a Mentor, Being a Mentor* (Eugene, OR: Harvest House, 2001), 78–79. Carolyn Mahaney addressed a related idea speaking on John 21:18-24 at The Gospel Coalition Women's Conference 2012 in Orlando. In her session titled, "The Snare of Compare," she called women to follow God's plan for them individually, without being sidetracked by what He has planned for others.

"For by the grace given me I say to every one of you: Do not think of yourself more highly than you ought, but rather think of yourself with sober judgment, in accordance with the measure of faith God has given you" (Rom. 12:3).

Therefore, in the context of modeling, it is helpful to keep in mind that we have each been given unique gifts from our Heavenly Father. Yes, we are all expected to meet the prerequisites that were discussed in Chapter Two; but please do not fall prey to comparing your weaknesses to another's strengths. It is counterproductive to seek to be someone else or to try to excel in someone else's areas of gifting. Focus your modeling on what is necessary for your mentee, and also on areas where God has gifted you. Keep in mind that your mentee can receive training and benefit from what is modeled by other women too, who are gifted in areas that you are not. You do not need to be all things to her. In fact, it is a healthy safeguard and shows both humility and maturity on your part when you are able to sincerely and wholeheartedly encourage her to seek out other godly women who can be role models for her as well.

COMPONENTS OF MODELING

Not all mentoring fits tidily into neat little hour-long blocks or half-day compartments. Nor should it, necessarily. You will find there is a lot of freedom as we move into our discussion of the components of a modeling approach. There are many ways to go about this job of training our younger women and supporting them in the process of growing to maturity in Christ. When you are starting out, though, too much freedom may be as overwhelming as too many guidelines. Too many options may be as overwhelming as having no idea where to begin. Having a list of components from which to choose, however, can provide a helpful starting place; and descriptions of the various components can help provide a clearer idea of what to do or what *could* be done.

We have established that mentoring is about shaping lives and making disciples. It is about behavioral change and changes in thinking. It is about getting younger women back on track. We are now about to see that this can be approached in many ways and accomplished by many means. We have just been reminded that each of us has been given a different set of gifts and life experiences by our Lord, and the gifts God has given us, and the experiences He has specifically planned for us contribute to making each of us unique individuals. "Just as each of us has one body with many members, and these members do not all have the same function, so in Christ we who are many form one body, and each member belongs to all the others. We have different gifts, according to the grace given us" (Rom. 12:4-6).

Each of these will affect not only the areas we focus on in our modeling, but will also impact the components of modeling that we choose to utilize. Do not feel like you need to try to implement every idea, approach, or method suggested. Rather, I invite you to view the two sections on components (modeling components and session components) as resources. As you choose an approach and select the components you will implement, you have the opportunity to personalize things. Seek God's guidance throughout the process. Bathe every decision in prayer. When we seek God earnestly, He will be found. Even in these seemingly small choices, we should ask Him to fill us with the knowledge of His will through all spiritual wisdom and understanding (Col. 1:9), and believe that He will do it. As you grow in your role and in your relationship with your mentee, and practice seeking God's guidance and wisdom as to what is best for you, you will become more comfortable forging your own unique plan.

Five basic components of the modeling approach are modeling a devotional life, modeling life skills, modeling everyday life, modeling ministry skills, and talking.

Model a Devotional Life

"Look away…they're communin'!" This line was spoken in a lazy southern drawl by a hillbilly on an episode of The Andy Griffith Show. The speaker was referring to a couple kissing. It was both amusing and accurate at the same time. Communing carries connotations of closeness, intimacy, and a deeper level of communication. It is "talking together, usually with profound intensity, intimacy, etc.; it refers to an interchange of thoughts or feelings."[49] It is not an everyday word these days. Neither is "devotional."

If we are going to model a devotional life, we should have a solid grasp of what it is. So, what is a "devotional life" anyway? It is a time that is set aside and devoted to communing with God, that is, being in intimate communication with Him. It will generally include time spent in God's Word and in prayer, as these are the primary ways that we converse with Him. Why is devotional life first on the list of things to model? Our relationship with God is our lifeline. This is true for mentor and mentee alike. Regular meaningful communication with God must be established and maintained for our spiritual life to continue. Learning how to remain connected to God through hearing from Him daily in Scripture and speaking with Him daily in prayer is absolutely essential. It is nonnegotiable.

The challenge is that our own personal devotional time is a personal thing. This time spent in prayer and the Word is usually a private affair, often done apart from even our own family members. To model this for a mentee, we will need to be intentional. One veteran suggests actually meeting with a "young friend" for a specified number of times to demonstrate how a devotional time is spent. If needed, she recommends providing a wake-up call or even taking a cup of coffee by a student's dorm room to help her get up for devotions! Once the daily habit is established, she suggests a brief weekly meeting together to share what has been learned.[50] This sounds both thorough and fantastic! However, we are not all full time ministry workers who live close to the ones we are shepherding. Meeting daily for a week may be daunting, overwhelming, or even impossible for many of us. Thankfully, modeling a devotional life effectively can be accomplished in fewer, less concentrated modeling sessions as well. And support, encouragement, and accountability can be offered through the use of phone calls, emails, or text messages to bridge the gap between times when you can meet together.

---

[49] "Communing." Dictionary.com. Online: http://www.dictionary.com/browse/communing. Accessed July 14, 2015.
[50] Fryling, *Disciplemakers' Handbook*, 160.

Wayne Cordeiro outlines a method of holding group devotions that effectively teaches and models one aspect of communing with God personally. While teaching personal devotions in a group setting may seem odd initially, it is actually an ingenious approach. First of all, it offers accountability in the area of reading God's Word, since the reading is done together. It is "together" in the sense that the group is gathered together while each person reads silently for twenty minutes, following their own individual Bible reading plan. In this way, it also encourages personal commitment and the establishment of a personal routine.

Secondly, his approach allows for built in assessment of how each person is progressing in the areas of hearing from God and making application to their own life. Following the time spent reading individually, twenty minutes is spent in personal journal writing focused on one truth God is speaking from all they have just read. Including a personal application made from that truth is encouraged. Then, during the final twenty minutes each individual shares what they have written with the whole group. Participants are also encouraged to write a short prayer at the end of their written journal entry, but the main focus of the hour is on hearing from God. This brief glimpse of Cordeiro's approach has been greatly simplified. The method is described fully in *The Divine Mentor*,[51] and is an approach that can easily be adapted for use with one mentee.

Speaking to God in prayer is the other important part of a devotional life. It will need to be modeled well, and it will need to be modeled over an extended period of time. Modeling is, in fact, the best method for teaching much of what needs to be taught about prayer. Even in a session approach, I recommend using modeling for teaching prayer. However, both initially and periodically, some biblical teaching on prayer will be needed as well.

There is no biblical directive that our focused prayer time should follow time in the Word, but this seems logical to recommend for at least one reason. Scripture guides our thinking, transforms and reshapes our thoughts, and prepares us to be able to pray according to God's

---

[51] Wayne Cordeiro, *The Divine Mentor* (Bloomington, MN: Bethany House, 2007), 147–148.

will. Our best prayers are often in response to what He has spoken to our hearts through His Word. In much of Scripture we see a pattern of God initiating and His people responding. He creates; we respond with praise. We see His holiness; we respond with worship. We see His standards and respond with prayers for His help to live up to them so that we can please Him, or confession for our failure to do so. We are aware of His power and His promises, and so we come to Him in prayer in our times of need.

Modeling a devotional time provides an opportunity both to teach and to correct misunderstandings, whether these are misunderstandings about God's Word, God's person, or about how we should relate to the Creator of the Universe, who is also our Heavenly Father.

Model Life Skills

"We finally just gave it away." His favorite shirt sat in the closet, unworn but longed for, for many months until the truth finally had to be acknowledged. It really never would be mended; she didn't know how. I've seen husbands give up waiting in such cases, and do the job themselves...if *they* know how. It may not seem that complicated to sew on buttons, mend a rip, or take up a hem, but at some point each of these skills has to be taught and learned before they can be used. The same is true of something as seemingly simple as ironing. Somehow, despite all the efforts to dispense with gender roles, it still seems to reflect on the wife when her husband appears in the public eye in a crumpled shirt.

The list of life skills that could be modeled for a mentee is almost endless. It would include activities such as a variety of cooking and baking skills, home management skills, organizational skills, space and time management tips, and budgeting. Perhaps your mentee needs some help learning how to disciple her children, or how to train and discipline them biblically. You may explore home remedies for caring for a sick family member, emergency procedures, or the vast worlds of gardening, nutrition, or food preservation together. She may join you on a cleaning day, or a canning day, or as you prepare for house or dinner guests. She may offer much needed help to you when you have a sick child or an injured husband, all the while learning from you how to care for her own in the future.

We often find meal preparation and entertaining on the list of life skills needed for running a home. Certainly planning and making nutritious meals is an important part of being busy at home and caring for a husband, children, other family members, and guests. But does your mentee know how to use hospitality or entertaining to intentionally deepen relationships or to reach out to visiting missionaries, lost neighbors, or members of your church family who may be lonely or struggling in other ways? Does she have a heart to want to learn how?

How are her basic cleaning abilities, home maintenance skills, organizational skills, and budgeting skills? These things matter because they impact the well-being of her family, the smooth functioning of her home, and the atmosphere there as well. How is she with minor home repairs; can she do some of these herself? Does she know how to go about finding a trustworthy repairman? From this sampling you can readily see that really any number of skills that relate to loving one's husband and children, working at home, submitting to one's husband, being kind, self-controlled (sensible), and pure (Titus 2) could be modeled and taught.

Stay Focused

As you can see, your assigned task could become very broad and far-reaching. You will need to remain focused on your specific goal. Your goal is not to fill time with activities! Remember, you are not called to be all things to your mentee. You are not going to learn how to do a certain task you cannot do or develop a specific skill you do not currently have in order to teach her.[52] Your primary task is to keep calling her back to God's standards and priorities. You are getting her back on track so that she obeys all that Jesus commanded. You want her to look like Jesus, so that she shows by her transformed life the power

Your goal is not to fill time with activities

---

[52] This is not to say you will never choose to learn something together, especially if it is something you really should know how to do.

that God has to change everyday people like you and like her. You have been assigned a clear goal, and you do not want to be sidetracked, so you must plan with intent how you will set about reaching that goal. Throughout all of your planning you must seek God's wisdom and direction. And then, you must follow through with your plans.

Modeling does require spending a lot of time together. Modeling how to disciple children, for example, may involve your mentee being present when you are having devotions with your children or grandchildren. You might invite her to listen in on conversations with them about the things of the Lord, or just observe how you naturally bring God into everyday conversations. You cannot always plan these sorts of conversations, however, and sometimes the most memorable ones occur when you least expected them to. For these reasons, you will sometimes need to repeat conversations and recount experiences for your mentee's benefit. In her book, *To Train Up A Child,* Debi Pearl shares about various times in her own life when she modeled the training of a child.[53] Such "second-hand modeling" could be very helpful for many mothers just starting out today.

This is also a biblical idea. Despite all the modeling the apostle Paul did himself, we still see him drawing on the good examples of others, holding them up as models to be emulated. For you, too, modeling will sometimes include recounting for your mentee what you modeled in her absence, or sharing with her the good examples that have been modeled by others.

> *And now, brothers, we want you to know about the grace that God has given the Macedonian churches. Out of the most severe trial, their overflowing joy and their extreme poverty welled up in rich generosity. For I testify that they gave as much as they were able, and even beyond their ability. Entirely on their own, they urgently pleaded with us for the privilege of sharing in this service to the saints. And they did not do as we expected, but they gave themselves first to the Lord and then to us in keeping with God's will.* (2 Cor. 8:1-5)

---

[53] Michael and Debi Pearl, *To Train Up A Child* (Pleasantville, TN: No Greater Joy Ministries, 2002), 4–10. This is not an endorsement for this book.

Model Everyday Life

Modeling aspects of everyday life makes sense as part of the training process. More importantly, we have seen that it is scriptural. The apostle Paul asked believers to remember how he lived among them; he urged his mentees to imitate him as he imitated Christ. And our Lord Himself exemplified this, utilizing this method throughout his life on earth. In *Heart to Heart with Pastors' Wives,* Gail MacDonald shares that observing a mentor in real life situations can be a key component of mentoring. "Most of what women learn from you will be picked up through observing your attitudes and reactions to everyday life. Christ fleshed out in us—what a hope! The rewards are immense."[54] This gets at the heart of modeling everyday life beautifully, even though our understanding of the concept of *sophronizo* will lead us to use the word "much" instead of "most." Certainly, however, we can agree that a little authenticity goes a long way in backing up our teaching! As mentors, our attitudes and actions do speak loudly, and our mentees will always learn from them, for better or worse. So although correction, instruction, encouragement, and accountability will be necessary for fulfilling our job as mentors, we can also readily see that there are some things that will be far more effectively communicated, understood, and learned through doing them together with our mentees than could ever be accomplished through many, many lectures.

Modeling everyday life will require spending a good deal of time together. If your mentee is to see you modeling life, you will need to "live life" together. Branch out. Allow your mentee to see you interact with the public, share the gospel with the lost, deal with delicate situations. Let her see you relating to your husband, children, relatives, and neighbors. Allow her to observe as you pour out your heart like water for your children's needs in prayer (Lam. 2:19), as you wrestle through hurts or challenges, and as you carry other's burdens to the Lord in intercessory prayer. Invite her to join you and support you. Welcome her, likewise, to join with you when you rejoice in God's blessings and in answered prayers.

---

[54] Gail MacDonald, "Chapter Nine, Mentoring: Woman to Woman," in *Heart to Heart with Pastor's Wives,* ed. Lynne Dugan (Ventura, CA: Regal, 1994), 101.

Some areas where you are weak or less practiced can be left for others to model for your mentee. Other areas need to be worked on so that you can be a good example. Because we have had so many health issues in our family, I found myself well prepared to model caring for special dietary needs for one mentee...including her own! Instead of observing me flustered or totally unable to care for her, because God had prepared me in advance, she could instead witness an example of how to adapt, accommodate, and roll with the punches. If accommodating special dietary needs is not a skill familiar to you, you may opt to leave that for someone else to teach your mentee.

Sharing the good news of salvation with others, on the other hand, is something that should be a part of the life of every believer. By God's handiwork in me, for most of my life it has been my normal practice to look for ways to share about Jesus in conversation whenever we have a service person in our home. Because this was my regular routine, if a mentee was present, she would be able to see this. If it didn't happen naturally despite my intentionality, then she would most likely see me head for the basket in the powder room and emerge with a gospel tract. She would hear, "Thanks again so very much. Can I share this with you as a thank you?" She would see a genuine smile. If this is not your usual practice, chances are it won't happen naturally and your mentee will not see you do this. You will model most effectively those things that are a genuine and customary part of your life.

Who would imagine that a thirty-minute wait on a living room couch could have had such an impact? Perfectly clear blue skies, bright sunshine, and brilliant white snow more than made up for the cold air outside, as Elspeth arrived early for an afternoon book study. Lunch had been cleared away, but Marty and I had been just about to pray together when she arrived. This was our practice most weekdays, before he headed back up to work at the seminary. We relocated to the bedroom to pray, leaving Elspeth alone to wait. The others in the study would arrive shortly. If anything, it seemed less than hospitable. It was some time later that I learned how God had ministered to her through this experience. That Marty and I loved one another was already known, but the idea that we took the time each day to pray together for one another, our children, and others touched Elspeth deeply, as did the evidence that this time we shared together with God was a priority. Her own parents' marriage was not like this. In fact, she had been wondering if she really wanted to get married herself, based on what she had seen in her own "Christian home."

At times we plan and model specific activities and skills, but sometimes when we least expect it, the light of our devotion to God still shines out to visibly brighten the way for someone following close behind. This light gave Elspeth hope that day, hope that perhaps she didn't need to fear marriage, hope that with God's help her own life did not have to follow her parents' pattern. This is why the qualification of piety is so important. It has to be who we are when we are alone, when no one is watching, and when we are unaware of who is watching.

She saw me as I pitched in and participated from a distance. Our son had arranged with a group of college friends to go to the closest city to witness. They planned to pass out copies of the Gospel of John and Christmas gospel tracts, and share more in conversations as they had opportunity. Their wonderful intentions filled my heart with joy. This was new to all of them. I wanted to support them. I realized they were about to engage in battle and needed to prepare for it, and that time with God would be the best way for Him to prepare and equip them. Through my son, I shared a resource with them in the form of a series of guided questions based on Scripture.

She observed as the group welcomed the resource, the suggestion that a time of reflection, confession, and supplication was an important part of preparing to go, and the offer of our basement as a quiet place to use for this purpose. She observed as I had a warm meal and hot drinks ready when the group returned later that cold evening to debrief this first effort with my husband and me. She had a front row seat for her observations—she was a part of the group herself. Remember that your mentee is learning from you how to treat and relate to others, not only from how you treat those others, but from how you treat and relate to her as well.

Participate in Ministry Together

Enormous high-powered fans from the fire department, large rolls of heavy black plastic, and a large salmon carcass—bones, fins, and scaly skin—all squeezed into our van, along with the team of high school girls. We were off to hold an outreach event among the underprivileged children in the nearest city. This month, we would be telling the story of Jonah while sitting inside a reconstructed black plastic "whale."

***

Jules and I drove first to one nursing home, and then to another. At the first, we picked up Anna. Her nursing home offered no opportunity for Christian fellowship around God's Word. At the second, we held a worship service where she was our guest, able to sing hymns, enjoy fellowship with friends she had not seen for years, and stay for a delicious dinner afterwards. We then wheeled her back to the car, loaded up her wheelchair, and returned her "home."

The first step in participating in ministry together is modeling ministry. The pattern we saw in the section on serving together was observation, partnership, and then supervised, independent ministry. Prayer and instruction should accompany each stage, from preliminary preparations to the final debriefing. It would seem logical that for this component, you should focus on ministries that you are able to model well and your mentee is able to learn. Pastor's wife Gail MacDonald shares, "Most of my mentoring relationships have involved learning how to be partners in a shared task. Such opportunities might include ministry to the homeless, remedial reading, Habitat for Humanity, care-giving or helping others study the Scriptures. The latter two have been where I have invested the greatest number of years."[55]

But what if your main area of ministry is a highly specialized one and your mentee is not called to or gifted in the same area? Or conversely, what if you are more of a crow and your mentee a nightingale? Don't let this concern you unduly. If your current areas of ministry do not naturally align, you have a few options. You may decide to choose another area to engage in together with your mentee, perhaps a broader area of service, one which all believers are called to embrace. There are many areas of need in our world and many ways you can serve together

---

[55] Gail MacDonald, Chapter Nine, Mentoring: Woman to Woman, in *Heart to Heart with Pastor's Wives*, 100.

to meet them. Another option would be to focus your mentoring on other areas besides partnering in ministry together. Remember, these components are offered as helpful, biblically-based *possibilities*; they are not mandatory. A third option would be to recruit another godly woman to fill this role for your mentee. However, in cases such as that of the crow and the nightingale, there is more to the story.

It may be true enough that you would not be the best model of the technical aspects of singing. Despite this, however, if you meet the biblical qualification of piety, there will still be much that you can teach and even model for your mentee that will help her to minister more effectively to others through music. You see, several things are considerably more important than the specifics of what you actually do in ministry together.

First, is the issue of focus. There is great benefit in helping your mentee to focus her energies on *others* through actually serving or ministering, rather than allowing herself to be occupied with more self-focused pursuits. The natural

Train your mentee to participate in every kind of ministry for the right reasons...

default is to fill our time with things that are focused on bringing us pleasure. Ministering to others is one good way to counter this.

Second, ministering together provides a wonderful opportunity to highlight the importance of humility. Is your mentee willing to lower herself, as Jesus did (see Phil. 2:5-8), and serve in whatever way God desires? Take advantage of the opportunity ministering together affords you to model for your mentee how to serve with humility.

Third, you should also train your mentee to participate in every kind of ministry for the right reasons. Ministry is to be done for God's glory and for the benefit of others, particularly the building up of the body of Christ and the salvation of the lost. Engaging in ministry should never be for our own glory, affirmation, or for what we can get out of it. This is a greater temptation in some areas of service than in others, but we should be alert to carefully guard against it always.

Some of these priorities can be best instilled through combining instruction, correction, and intentional accountability with the modeling. For others, more can be gained through the experience of joint participation than could ever be accomplished through many lectures. For example, the delight and challenges of honoring our elders may not be readily apparent from the knowledge that we *ought* to do this. Talking about the value of hospital visitation is one thing, and you may even be inspired to do likewise as I share about the opportunities this has given me for witnessing to others over the years. However, when I invite you to come with me and two others, and I pack a fancy tea pot, four tea cups, several tea choices, and home-baked desserts, and we arrive in Anna's shared hospital room for a tea party, you will come away with a totally different picture. As you sit on the closed porta-potty for lack of other seating, cloth napkin tucked delicately into your collar, the experience is your own. As you take in the expression of genuine appreciation written across Anna's face, and hear the patient in the other bed get in on the conversation…and attention, you are a firsthand witness as to how this scenario often unfolds.

I loved Anna. When I first met her, she lived independently. We met in her home for missions committee meetings. In the decade plus that ensued, I followed her from hospital to nursing home to care facility after care facility. Whenever God led, I took someone with me—not always for Anna, or for me; sometimes it was for that person's own benefit.

"You want me to cover your shift so you can do what?*" The other Residence Hall Assistant could not understand why Char wanted to miss her scheduled duty. What appeal could there possibly be in having dinner with a group of old ladies in the home of a middle-aged one? Having never experienced one of these herself, Char couldn't offer a very satisfying response. When she returned later that night, however, her eyes glowed as she said simply, "It was an enchanted evening. I wished it would never end." She had been in the company of some of the community's unsung spiritual giants, women in their 80s and 90s who had lived long and hard for Jesus. True, they were now fading in varying degrees and in different ways, but through course after sumptuous course, across the twinkle of what could have been a hundred candles on the elegantly laid table, Char's fellowship with these women had been rich—a memory she said she would treasure forever.*

Describing an activity or behavior to a mentee is one thing. Inviting her to actively participate in it or to observe it firsthand is another thing entirely.

Engage in Conversation

A modeling approach still calls for conversations that allow you to reflect, explain, challenge, instruct, debrief, and so forth. Again, seeking God's wisdom and direction, have a plan for what you want to talk about. Utilize the suggestions listed for sessions. And even though your mentee may be focused on observing you, learning a skill from you, or participating in an activity with you, do not allow the entire conversation to focus on that skill exclusively. Our actions typically flow out of our beliefs. Our philosophy of life, or worldview, is critically important. Remember this and don't leave it up to your mentee to fill in the blanks. Take time to talk about these things. Explain why you do what you do; clarify your motives; identify the priorities and values that drive your decisions and behavior. Share with her how God has spoken to you and taught you in the areas you are currently focused on in your modeling. Point her back to Him, His standards, His love, and His power and desire to help her.

In a nutshell, these are some of the main elements that can be utilized in a modeling approach.

Chapter 7

A SESSION APPROACH

The session approach refers to mentoring that takes place primarily in the context of meetings. Each session is comprised of a variety of activities, and can be quite eclectic. This approach is probably best described by listing some of the possible components of a session. As I do so, keep in mind that it would be unusual for any one session to include every single component. Note also that it is normal for the time spent in a particular activity to vary from week to week. Some components should be a regular part of any given week; some will be included less frequently; and others may be engaged in only on occasion. The core components are prayer, sharing life, sharing God's Word, and offering accountability. Sharing life skills, encouraging ministry, and some modeling are examples of optional components that can be incorporated into sessions either regularly or occasionally.

Finally, beginning and ending each session well could also be considered separate components.

BIBLICAL BASIS

As with other features of biblical mentoring, Scripture is our guide for understanding how sessions are to work. Let's begin by establishing a biblical basis for the core components. The importance of prayer and the Word of God permeate Scripture:

All Scripture is God-breathed and is useful for teaching, rebuking, correcting and training in righteousness, so that the man of God may be thoroughly equipped for every good work. (2 Tim. 3:16-17)

Preach the Word; be prepared in season and out of season; correct, rebuke and encourage—with great patience and careful instruction. (2 Tim. 4:2)

And pray in the Spirit on all occasions with all kinds of prayers and requests. With this in mind, be alert and always keep on praying for all the saints. (Eph. 6:18)

Pray continually. (1 Thess. 5:17)

Be...faithful in prayer. (Rom. 12:12)

A biblical basis for sharing life together is found in 1 Thessalonians 2:8: "We loved you so much that we were delighted to share with you not only the gospel of God but our lives as well, because you had become so dear to us." Acts 2:42, 44-46 also paints for us a picture of sharing life:

They devoted themselves to the apostles' teaching and to the fellowship, to the breaking of bread and to prayer... [44]All the believers were together and had everything in common. [45]Selling their possessions and goods, they gave to anyone as he had need. [46]Every day they continued to meet together in the temple courts. They broke bread in their homes and ate together with glad and sincere hearts.

We have already seen that sharing life together is a prerequisite for developing the kind of relationship that is indispensable if a mentor is going to be able to help her mentee get back on track.

Providing accountability is one effective means a mentor can use to help establish her mentee on the narrow path that leads to life. Galatians 6:1 says, "Brothers, if someone is caught in a sin, you who are spiritual should restore him gently. But watch yourself, or you also may be tempted." Accountability can be a part of the restoration process. It can also be a preventative against relapses into sin or a safeguard against falling into new areas of temptation. James 5:19 reads, "My brothers, if one of you should wander from the truth and someone should bring him back, remember this: Whoever turns a sinner from the error of his way will save him from death and cover over a multitude of sins." Both of these passages offer a biblical reminder of the goal of accountability: the mentee's restoration. It is for her growth; it is for her to triumph over sin. It is for her good.

Often, a mentor may need to grow in this area of offering accountability. It may be unfamiliar or uncomfortable. She may have come to view any sort of confrontation or correction of sin as judgmental, and therefore to be avoided. She may have learned to equate addressing delicate issues with being impolite or politically incorrect. Additionally, providing accountability requires both humility and confidence on the part of the mentor. Initially, it may all just seem to be too daunting of a task, one a mentor may prefer to postpone or ignore altogether. Assistance may be needed to help a reticent mentor change her thinking. An in-depth study of the verses in the previous paragraph could be a very helpful starting point. Once a mentor has embraced this part of her role and is willing to learn how to discharge this duty, then through proper instruction, practice, and encouragement, she can be trained to do this. In time, she will be able to confidently, lovingly, and effectively offer accountability for her mentee.

Sometimes this accountability will come in the form of an exercise the mentee agrees to work on for a specified period of time. Sometimes it will take the form of a gentle question, and other times it will involve a face-to-face confrontation. Paul's face-to-face conversation with Peter held him accountable for his actions.

When Peter came to Antioch, I opposed him to his face, because he was clearly in the wrong. Before certain men came from James, he used to eat with the Gentiles. But when they arrived, he began to draw back and separate himself from the Gentiles because he was afraid of those who belonged to the circumcision group. The other Jews joined him in his hypocrisy, so that by their hypocrisy even Barnabas was led astray. (Gal. 2:11-13)

Sin that is not confronted will harm your mentee and dishonor God, and can lead others astray. Addressing sin and also assigning specific activities designed to target and eradicate sin are two of the ways mentors can offer accountability. Accountability exercises can be designed to either develop or decrease certain specific behaviors or attitudes. Accountability is a powerful way to keep a mentee from going astray; it is also a valuable tool for retraining her.

Is there a biblical basis for the other suggested components of an eclectic session? Sharing life skills is often a necessary part of equipping a mentee to obey God. A couple of passages speak to this. According to Titus 2:5, women are to be "busy at home" (NIV), "working at home" (ESV), "homemakers" (NKJV), or to "take care of their homes" (NLT). Managing a household requires many skills. Consider some of the activities presented as examples of good home management in Proverbs 31. This imaginary model homemaker selects wool and flax and works with eager hands. She brings her food from afar. She provides food for her family and for her maids. She considers a field and buys it; out of her earnings she plants a vineyard. She trades profitably. She makes coverings for her bed, linen garments to sell, and supplies merchants with sashes. Many of the skills women will need today have changed, but many skills are still required to discharge the responsibilities of a homemaker competently. As mentors, we should be willing to help our mentees in areas where they need the kind of help that we are able to provide.

Several passages speak of the importance of ministering and of encouraging others to minister:

Discharge all the duties of your ministry. (2 Tim. 4:5b)

Serve one another in love. (Gal. 5:13)

Each one should use whatever gift he has received to serve others... (1 Pet. 4:10)

I remind you to fan into flame the gift of God, which is in you through the laying on of my hands. (2 Tim. 1:6)

This brings us to the quasi components of beginning and ending well. "Beginning well" involves seeking God's wisdom and guidance and being as prepared as you can be for your session.

If any of you lacks wisdom, he should ask God, who gives generously to all without finding fault, and it will be given to him. (James 1:5)

Trust in the LORD with all your heart and lean not on your own understanding; in all your ways acknowledge him, and he will make your paths straight. (Prov. 3:5-6)

Whatever you do, work at it with all your heart, as working for the Lord, not for men. (Col. 3:23)

Applying these verses to our mentoring means that we will both prepare carefully for our mentoring sessions and ask for God's guidance and blessing as we begin. In the case of King Hezekiah of Judah, seeking God and working wholeheartedly led to God's blessing: "In everything that he undertook in the service of God's temple and in obedience to the law and the commands, he sought his God and worked wholeheartedly. And so he prospered" (2 Chron. 31:21).

Finally, as we consider the biblical basis for the "ending well" component, we will see that although it does include many personal ideas, these are guided by three general biblical principles. The first is giving thought to one's ways:

The wisdom of the prudent is to give thought to their ways, but the folly of fools is deception. (Prov. 14:8)

An upright man gives thought to his ways. (Prov. 21:29b)

Now this is what the LORD Almighty says: "Give careful thought to your ways." (Hag. 1:5)

Ending well provides the mentor and mentee with the opportunity to give thought to their ways together.

The second principle is committing one's ways to God (see Prov. 3:5-6 above). Proverbs 16:3 says, "Commit to the LORD whatever you do, and your plans will succeed." The act of committing our ways to God provides us with an opportunity to evaluate these ways according to His standards. We bring them before Him and they are exposed to His gaze, to the scrutiny of His standards as expressed in His Word. It is also an act of submission to His lordship. Finally, committing our ways to God represents an acknowledgment of our need for Him. This admission of our need can range in intensity from a request for His involvement to an urgent, passionate plea for His help.

The third guiding principle is purposing or resolving to do what is right. Many years ago I implemented the practice of "resolving," which I learned from the Puritan pastor Jonathan Edwards, into my own life. Over time, with God's help, it has produced much good fruit! As I look into Scripture, I see that long before Jonathan Edwards, God's people had discovered the power of this practice. In Psalm 17:3 the Psalmist shared, "Though you probe my heart and examine me at night, though you test me, you will find nothing; I have resolved that my mouth will not sin." Daniel, likewise, "resolved not to defile himself with the royal food and wine, and he asked the chief official for permission not to defile himself this way" (Dan. 1:8). Jehoshaphat "resolved to inquire of the LORD, and he proclaimed a fast for all Judah" (2 Chron. 20:3). And the apostle Paul "resolved to know nothing while [he] was with [the Corinthians] except Jesus Christ and him crucified" (1 Cor. 2:2). In each case, there was an action, an active decision to do or not do something. In each case, this action of resolving led to specific good behaviors and outcomes.

We will see how these three biblical principles of giving thought to our ways, committing our ways to God, and purposing to do what is right impact the working out of the "ending well" component when we develop and examine the idea more closely in the next section of this chapter.

A CLOSER LOOK AT SESSION COMPONENTS
Begin Well
Committing your time together to God in prayer is uncomplicated, but it is this very simplicity that may lead to it being entirely or occasion-

---

SESSION COMPONENTS

Although the following ideas are numbered, with the exception of 1, 9, and 10, this is not a list to progress through, checking off each item as you complete it. These are individual stand-alone ideas from which you can choose as you compose and arrange your own session.

1. Begin by seeking God.
2. Share about the past week.
3. Share God's Word.
4. Provide accountability.
5. Pray together.
6. Share life skills.
7. Encourage ministry.
8. Discuss homework or account-ability assignment.
9. End well.
10. Close in prayer.

---

ally overlooked. It is simple, but crucial. It would be natural to launch right in to sharing about what has happened in each of your lives in the time that elapsed since your last session. This may begin quite naturally from the moment you first meet one another at the front door or at the restaurant table. Determine to interrupt this conversation, if necessary, to converse with God. One mentor shared with me that she and her mentee engaged in more general conversation before placing their orders with the waitress, and reserved more serious matters for after the food had arrived when interruptions would be kept to a minimum and more focus and privacy would be afforded. If you are meeting in a restaurant, perhaps saying grace will be the time when you also commit your conversation to God, the signal that the mentoring session is beginning in earnest. Whether at home or elsewhere, plan to begin well. Make a point of praying together for God's presence and wisdom as you begin to meet each and every time. Sometimes we "have not" because we have not asked.

Share about the Past Week

It is not necessary for the sharing about each other's lives to be treated as a distinct component. You can certainly view it as one, but keep in mind that this sort of sharing will also typically happen naturally as you go through other components. In fact, you may actually need to set a limit on this time. You want to share, while also being careful not to take a lot of time just visiting about trivial matters. If one or both of you are loquacious, you will especially need to guard against important things getting crowded out at the end as a result of extended visiting about inconsequential matters earlier on.

Naturally, the mentee will share. Her life and growth are the focus. The mentor often also shares, however, as this provides an opportunity for her mentee to learn from her example. As she shares, her mentee catches a picture of how she uses her time, what she is learning, how she is dealing with challenges, how she is sharing her faith, and so on. Share what will meet a need in your mentee. Share what will build her up, challenge, or encourage her. Share something you have in common, perhaps your progress in an area you are both working on. If your mentee is shy or reticent to open up, you might need to help her in the process of sharing as well. You may gently, as appropriate, prompt her to give a general update on current life issues, joys, challenges, trials, areas where wisdom is needed, decisions that need to be made, progress in particular relationships, triumphs, what God has been teaching her that week, areas of concern, and so forth.

During this interaction, remember James 1:19. "My dear brothers, take note of this: Everyone should be quick to listen, slow to speak and slow to become angry." Do not say everything you know or everything you *could* say on any given topic. Jesus certainly didn't! Be selective, strategic, and intentional. Chit-chat can very easily get you far off track.

Keep the focus on your mentee's growth into Christlikeness. Listen carefully. Often God uses this time to direct you to topics that He wants to address in your mentee's life through you. Be discerning. As she shares, she will be revealing her heart. Asking some questions may help you to discern what she is facing and how she is viewing the situation herself. They may also help you to identify what her real needs are.

Does she need encouragement? Hope? Instruction? Admonition? Rebuke? Comfort? Redirection? Or just a listening ear? Be alert. Is she demonstrating humility or pride as she relates her past week's events? Is there evidence of forgiveness or is there lingering bitterness? Are there evidences of anger or hurt that need to be addressed? Perhaps you will be able to identify where the thinking of the world is surfacing and how you can lead her to recognize it for what it is. Can you lead her to see the differences between what she is saying, her current perspective on her life's situations, and what God's Word has to say about those same situations and how they should be viewed? Can you identify values and priorities that need to be realigned to God's standards and will?

Share God's Word

The Word of God is our lifeline. You want to model this in your mentoring sessions. This means that at least at some point during every session you will point your mentee to God's Word. This may include reading, studying, or memorizing God's Word together. Studying and memorizing Scripture tend to be more predictable or structured and require you to prepare ahead of time in specific ways. However, preparation is also necessary for the more informal ways of sharing God's Word together.

If you prefer a less structured approach than Bible study or memorization, there are several options to consider. First, you could include a time to answer any questions your mentee may have from her own personal reading of God's Word in the previous week. Another option would be to refer to Scripture as you answer any general questions she may have. Remember that if a mentee raises a question or life situation for which you have no sure or ready answer, "being slow to speak" means that you will humbly tell her so, and then look into finding one for her.

A third informal way to share God's Word together does not rely on questions. Rather, as your mentee shares, you simply direct her to God's Word and its application for a specific area of her life. This is an excellent way of showing her the absolute relevance of Scripture and how to apply God's Word naturally. Much good teaching occurs as you thoughtfully and intentionally respond to the life experiences she is sharing by directing her to Scripture. You can see from this that these less structured approaches require a solid grasp on Scripture to be effective; mentors will need a certain level of biblical literacy to be able to do this.

From time to time, you may also want to share with your mentee particular truths God has taught you from your own personal time in His Word during the week, along with any applications. Or you may choose to simply read a passage together when you meet, following this with discussion or sharing some additional teaching or application derived from it. Finally, there may be times when you will want to assign your mentee relevant passages to read and meditate on between sessions, which you would then revisit together during your next meeting.

With each of these suggestions, whether you opt for a formal or informal approach to sharing Scripture, keep in mind Jesus' example and the command in Ephesians 4:29: "Do not let any unwholesome talk come out of your mouths, but only what is helpful for building others up according to their needs, that it may benefit those who listen." Remember that Jesus did not share every verse He knew or all the helpful information He had. And neither should we. Had he done so, those around Him would have been completely overwhelmed! Sensitively, He followed both Ephesians 4:29, focusing on the needs of the hearer, and another constraint—the Father's will (John 12:49).[56] We should seek to do likewise, even when sharing insights from Scripture.

Provide Accountability

Providing accountability can be an important component of helping younger women get back on track. A person who is accountable has

---

[56] "For I did not speak of my own accord, but the Father who sent me commanded me what to say and how to say it" (John 12:49).

an obligation to report, explain, or justify something. In a mentoring relationship, where change in behavior is desired and expected, I would highly recommend getting a commitment to accountability up front. This agreement allows you to ask hard questions. It allows you to set practical behavioral assignments for your mentee designed to move her towards the goals outlined in Scripture and agreed on by both of you. It sets in clear view the expectation that you will be making demands, and that she is obligating herself to work towards meeting them. She will be reporting her progress to you. Sometimes this will be cause for praise and rejoicing as you thank God together for victories won; other times there may be need for reassurance, assistance, encouragement, or correction. As you design and implement accountability exercises, your mentee needs to be assured that you are working with her out of genuine love and with her best interests in mind.

So, either before or during the first session, ask your mentee for permission to hold her accountable. Thereafter, regularly ask her to report on the areas of accountability that you have agreed on. This could be one specific area worked on over an extended period of time, or it could be various individual weekly assignments. Do not neglect to ask for a progress report when you are working on a longer term project. The regular reporting is important. It serves two key functions: recording progress and providing motivation. Just knowing she will be giving an account can significantly motivate her as she works towards the goal. We are in good company in using accountability in this way, as this is one of the motivational techniques God our Father uses with us (see, e.g., Rom. 14:12; Heb. 4:13; 13:17; 1 Pet. 4:5). Many mentees will be less likely to invest the same degree of effort if they think they will not have to give an account. Additionally, knowing you will talk about this the next time you meet together helps her to keep the goals she is working towards in focus during the time that you are apart.[57]

Weekly assignments can be practical, behavioral, or more intellectual in nature. It depends on your current focus. Both studying truth and making changes in behaviors are crucial for increasing in maturity in Christ. In either case, knowing someone is going to ask you about what

---

[57] Van Atta, *Women Encouraging Women*, 57.

you did remains a strong motivator for performing challenging tasks. A regular component of a mentoring session should be checking on the progress of the last week's assignment or other ongoing issues. When a mentee consistently fails to live up to her part of the agreement, this could be a signal that some reevaluation is necessary. You may need to reexamine your joint goals, her level of commitment, or her ability to keep her commitment. In extreme cases, it may be necessary to rethink the whole mentoring relationship.

Pray Together

There are many reasons to spend time in prayer together each time you meet. Prayer is critical for maintaining our personal relationship with God. There are many truths and principles that can be taught about prayer—and this needs to be done if your mentee is not yet aware of them—but there is no substitute for actually praying with her. There is much about prayer that is best learned through modeling and participation.

Including many kinds of prayer when you pray together will benefit your mentee immensely. Suppose your mentee has only been accustomed to asking God to do things for her. Joint prayer time is a very natural and effective way to introduce her to prayers of praise, confession, and thanksgiving as well. It provides an opportunity to model such praying for her and it also provides a safe context where she can gain practice in praying in these ways herself. As her mentor you can model for her praying intercessory prayers, whether the actual prayers are for her or for others. You can also model for her how to pray according to God's will by using Scriptures to guide both your requests and your praise.

From time to time you may want to schedule an extended prayer time as the focus of your session. Choose a passage of Scripture, a single verse, or an attribute of God to focus your worship on. You may each also want to choose a verse to pray through for yourselves and for one another. Sometimes this verse can be a promise that is applicable to believers today; at other times, it may be a verse that communicates something God has commanded us to do.[58] You likely will not be able

---

[58] *Staying on Track: Equipping Women for Biblical Mentoring* has more on this.

to have an extended prayer time every week, but do plan on this at least occasionally.

As your mentee observes you relating to your Heavenly Father first hand, she will have the opportunity to see your heart from a different perspective than at any other time. Similarly, be aware that your most penetrating insights into your mentee may well come as you hear her praying with you. For these reasons, this is not a time you want to miss. Allocate some time to pray together each time you meet.

Teach Life Skills

Teaching specific life skills can be scheduled from time to time as part of a session approach. Aspects of this were discussed in the chapter on modeling. Teaching a mentee life skills will involve sharing information, modeling the processes, and helping her to gain experience, confidence, and some level of proficiency. The list of beneficial life skills that you could share during a session is almost endless. There should be a definite purpose behind what you do, and what you choose to teach her should be moving her towards fulfilling the overarching biblical goals of the Great Commission (disciples who obey everything Christ commanded), Colossians 1:28 (becoming perfect Christ followers), and Titus 2:4-5. Basically, any skills that enhance her ability to love her husband and children well, manage her home well, and relate to others well are clearly included in the job description outlined in Titus 2.

Encourage Ministry

This has a slightly different flavor than the ministering together component of the modeling approach, but the same heart and goal. In a session approach, you can begin by simply sharing naturally about any ministries in which you are involved.

…when you list ministries, include good works for which women in particular are commended in Scripture…

If your mentee is involved in ministry, encourage her to share about those experiences from time to time, and pray with her about them. Support her as appropriate and as you are able. If you become aware that she needs redirection, take the time to prayerfully address that.

If she is not involved in ministry herself, seek God's guidance with her in prayer as she explores where He may have her serve Him. He may lead you to introduce her to some possibilities for which she may be suited or gifted, or in which she may be interested. Or, He may direct her to an area where she will be totally out of her comfort zone and completely dependent on Him. Be sure to include a variety of good works in your list of ministry opportunities, especially those for which women in particular are commended in Scripture. Remember that sometimes these will not be included in the list of ministries your local church sponsors.

Once she has found her niche, as you are able, help her develop or improve her ministry skills. Remember that helping her does not mean that you have to do it yourself. It may involve enlisting the help of someone else or recommending a class or a person to take her under her wing for that specific purpose. Throughout the process, you should encourage her, support her, and provide feedback. Teach her to minister for the purpose of bringing glory to God, and not for gaining gratitude or praise for herself.

Discuss Homework or Accountability Assignment

In each session you will want to schedule time to assign and discuss the current homework or accountability assignment, whether it is a new or an ongoing one. Allow enough time to explain it clearly so that your mentee knows exactly what she is committing to work on between sessions. The assignment should keep her growth and the goals you are targeting in focus for her while you are apart.

Depending on your relationship with your mentee, and taking into account your respective maturity levels and even your personality types, assignments may be created by the mentor, by the mentee, or by both women through joint consultation. If you are creating the assignment, be clear as you explain it. Invite questions for clarification, and when appropriate be open to modifications.

Sometimes a mentee will come up with excellent long- and short-term goals, assignments, and projects on her own. If this has not been the case with your mentee, but you feel this is something she is capable of, discuss the possibility with her openly. Then, each week gently prompt her to follow through. "Which of the behaviors or issues that we spoke about today would you like to target to work on this week? How do you think you can work on this? What changes would you like to implement?" And so forth. If she needs more guidance or assistance, try asking, "Would you be open to trying this activity? Are you willing to commit to doing this or avoiding that?"

Not infrequently, it is in the very moment, as you are talking with her, that God will guide you to the perfect idea to solidify the concept He is teaching her. This was the case with a pastor's wife a few years ago. This sweet young wife and mother was not a regular mentee, but had attended a study I taught previously and had then asked to meet with me for an individual session or two. The issue at hand was that in their marriage and parenting one spouse was more lenient and affirming, and the other more of a disciplinarian and quicker to see issues that needed to be addressed. For one week both agreed to intentionally switch roles from their own natural tendencies and instead do what their spouse would normally do. This exercise proved to be very enlightening. It forced each to see things from the other's perspective, and led each to gain empathy for the other. This dear husband and wife each saw how they both were needed and how they both actually worked together. This increased their appreciation for one another, while also encouraging a tempering of their own traits. The exercise served to increase their unity and solidarity. This was an assignment inspired by God in the midst of the session. He has led me in similar ways repeatedly in the past, and I believe He would delight to do the same for you too.

End Well
Ending well is important. Some key elements of ending well are reviewing together what transpired in your session, asking key questions, and engaging in informal evaluation. If it is at all possible, do not conclude by just sharing the next assignment and a closing prayer.

A great deal can be solidified during these last few minutes together. This is one of the reasons I highly recommend you review together what you have covered in your session before parting ways. This can be done effectively by orally composing a bullet-style list together of what transpired, recapping the various components with a word or phrase, or by summarizing what was discussed in a sentence or two. I like to follow this by asking one of my favorite closing questions: What will you take away from our time together today? These two activities in and of themselves are often all it takes to cement the content, underscore the value, and pinpoint the highlights of the session.

As time permits, you can also explore other issues, such as, "What additional questions did our time together raise?" Jot these down for next time. "Are there additional things besides what is addressed in this week's assignment that you would like to work on coming out of today's meeting?" Again, write down any responses. These could become accountability assignments sometime in the future. If one relates to a more urgent or time sensitive issue, it could even be added to the previously assigned homework or used to replace it. "Were any new thoughts or issues raised today that you would like to focus on more next time?" If so, an awareness of this may direct you, as the mentor, to engage in a particular Bible study during the week to prepare for your next session.

Ending well cements what has transpired. It can inspire the application of truths; it can inspire further study; it can provide direction for future planning. You can also use these closing moments to evaluate your session together and decide if you want to make changes in how you use your time or how you relate to one another in the future. These are just some of the reasons I recommend that you do not skip the review time. Try to monitor your time so that you don't run out and miss out on this component. Personally, I have not only found this brief recapping time to be very beneficial, but I genuinely sense its loss when we don't gauge our time well and it has to be omitted.

Close in Prayer

A closing prayer can be as short as a few sentences that take less than a minute, thanking God for His presence and insights given. It could also be a longer time used to commit issues or requests that stem from the mentoring session to God. It may be the first time that you ask God's help for the specific assignment your mentee will be focusing on in the coming days. Whether it includes all or none of these, prayer brings closure to your session and is actually the final step of ending well.

THROUGHOUT THE SESSION

The following pointers are not linked to any particular component, but rather are activities that can be used at any time throughout the session. The first is sharing from your own life experiences. Whenever it is appropriate you may feel led to share things that could meet a need your mentee has or encourage her. Share trials, victories, lessons learned, wisdom gained, tips for life, practical advice, times you failed and tried again, and times God enabled you to persevere. Share about your personal walk with the Lord: answered prayers and how Scripture spoke to you, convicted you, or comforted you.

The second pointer is to use questions skillfully. You may use them to help clarify what your mentee is sharing, to help your mentee figure out what to do in a certain situation, or to devise an effective plan of action. Your skillful use of questions may be employed to help her see herself or her circumstances accurately. Skillful questions will sometimes help her to get past her blind spots in a way that direct confrontation will not, enabling her to see for herself what her real needs are. Many times you will need to use a *series* of questions to gently reveal her sin or errors, so that she sees for herself where she went wrong, and is willing to call sin sin. At other times skillful questions may be needed to help her see her own progress or worth, strengths or gifts.[59]

A third activity that occurs throughout a session is answering your mentee's questions and concerns. These may be questions from life situations or from her devotional times. We touched on this in the "Share God's Word" component; however, questions may arise at any time throughout the session. When appropriate, find answers together in God's Word. This models for her how to go about doing this for herself. And again, when you don't know the answers or where to find them readily, you will need to seek help yourself. Be humble enough to admit this. She needs to see humility modeled too.

---

[59] More on the use of questions is included in *Staying on Track: Equipping Women for Biblical Mentoring.*

Finally, be appropriate in your responses and communication. As God tells us in 1 Thessalonians 5:14, "And we urge you, brothers, warn those who are idle, encourage the timid, help the weak, be patient with everyone." It would be wrong to help the idle or to encourage them in their idleness. Similarly, the weak and timid do not need warning; they need help and encouragement. As much as you are able, offer the response that will lead your mentee toward becoming perfect in Christ. Spiritual maturity is the goal.[60]

We have considered ten possible components for an eclectic mentoring session. Remember, as we conclude this chapter, that a session could be comprised of just two or three of them. Or perhaps you will touch on several briefly, but focus the majority of your time on just one or two. When you are starting out, allow yourself time to explore. Even after you have some experience, you can still give yourself the freedom to be flexible and change things up. These are ideas and suggestions. It is not better to do more or worse to do less. Each mentoring pair is unique, and circumstances are always changing. As always, seek God's guidance. He is so faithful to respond.

---

[60] The idea of reading cues and responding appropriately is also developed further in *Staying on Track: Equipping Women for Biblical Mentoring.*

Chapter 8

BOOK STUDIES
AND THE BEREAN CALL

WHERE HAVE ALL THE BIBLE STUDIES GONE?

Step aside, Bible Study! Enter the "Take Over of the Book Study"! Book studies have become exceedingly popular today. The concept, however, is nowhere to be found in Scripture. By "book study" I am referring to the practice of reading a book and discussing its contents, often with the aid of study questions provided by the author. In many churches, book studies have almost completely replaced genuine Bible studies, where men and women study the Word of God for themselves. It is sadly not uncommon to find that in a list of "Bible Study" options offered in a women's program all the choices listed are book studies and not one is an actual study of the Bible itself. Although each of these books is ostensibly written by a Christian author, studying a book is clearly not the same as studying God's inspired, inerrant, infallible Word.

DOING A BOOK STUDY IS NOT MENTORING

A book study can be one component of a more comprehensive mentoring program, but by itself a book study is not mentoring. It is not mentoring even if the book is soundly based on Scripture. It is not mentoring even if it addresses an area in a mentee's life where she needs to be called back on track. A book study is

By itself a book study is not mentoring.

especially not mentoring if the relationship between the women will end when the book ends. This signals that the goal was completing the book, not "completing" the mentee. However, although using book studies is a far cry from being a complete approach to mentoring, they can certainly still be a valuable tool for mentors.

PROS AND CONS

One reason book studies may have become so popular today is that usually the "work" of teaching has been done by someone else, namely the book's author. Those participating in the study need only to read the material and interact with it, not create it. This can be a huge benefit to busy women. It can also, though, keep women from receiving the benefits that only come from doing the work that is necessary to study a topic themselves. If the book contains errors, these are multiplied among those who lack discernment or who fail to take the time to examine the content and evaluate it against Scripture. Having said all of this, if carefully chosen books containing sound teaching are used, book studies can be quite beneficial. They also have another huge advantage: They essentially provide a third person, in the form of the author, to address potentially sticky or sensitive issues "objectively." At times, this can be a very valuable benefit indeed.

CAUTIONS AND PRECAUTIONS

I cannot, however, with a clear conscience offer even the slightest endorsement of book studies without sharing a number of cautions and issuing a strong call to be "Bereans." Before we make the decision to use any book, it is imperative that we ascertain that it is a *good* book.

What the author is proposing needs to be solidly based on Scripture. And I don't mean that the author has sprinkled references to Scripture throughout the book. There should be no doubt whatsoever that what is being taught is biblical.

As we move into this cautionary section, my singular motivation is to guard and strengthen the sheep, the people of God. God calls his people sheep for a reason. It is extremely easy for sheep to be led astray. A little yeast affects a whole lot of dough; or in other words, just a small bit of wrong teaching can have huge and devastating effects. I mean that! Just ask Tracy, whose whole church was torn apart as a result of teaching that was introduced by an undiscerning pastor's wife as she taught the women of the church. This teaching next spread to the pulpit and eventually culminated in a painful church split from which it will be difficult for many to ever fully recover. Not every grain of yeast has this effect, but the same potential is present in every single granule. It does not take a lot of error to do the job. Lies and falsehood are potent weapons; every misguided idea and each false assertion packs a powerful punch. The way missionary Paul Washer drove this point home was memorable for me: "Do you know how to make highly effective rat poison? It requires ninety-eight percent really good rat food…and just two percent poison!" My recollection of the numbers may not be exact, but the point was well taken.

When it comes to book studies written by Christian authors, there is a very strong temptation to trust others far too easily, even blindly. This includes those who have studied the Bible or theology more than you have; those who hold a title or occupy a position that implies they should know more than you do about spiritual matters; those who have written a book or started a program or ministry; or sometimes even those who have simply done the work for you to free you up! If we are going to take advantage of the beneficial book study resources that are available, we will need to be responsible. We will need to read with discernment so that we identify books with poison and reject them, and only use books that are clearly anchored in the truth and that will nourish our souls and lead us and our mentees into righteousness.

It is for this reason I say to you, "Reading critically is critically important!" Write this down on the flyleaf of your next book. Memorize it.

Practice it. The foundation of our lives should be God's authoritative Word. Unfortunately, too many times, opinions get shared as if they were God's Word. Advice in popular books far too commonly echoes the thinking of the world. Instead of sharing the thinking that surrounds them, Christian authors must share insights of a renewed mind that is fixed on things above. They must share eternal values and perspectives. They should, but they do not always succeed at this. It is for this reason that I urge you to become Berean women. Acts 17:11 tells us, "Now the Bereans were of more noble character than the Thessalonians, for they received the message with great eagerness *and examined the Scriptures every day to see if what Paul said was true*" (emphasis added). This was the apostle Paul they were checking up on! And he commended them for it. I am inviting you to join me in doing likewise. Right now, I encourage you to write out this verse, memorize it, and then begin to live out the example of the Bereans.

EVALUATING BOOKS

When we set out to evaluate a book, how do we go about it? Where do we begin? How will we know when it is off track, and when it is trustworthy? What criteria will we use?

One of our goals as Christian women and as mentors is to be more discerning, so that we are better able to evaluate what we are told and what we read, weighing it all against God's Word. Your best strategy for becoming a better Berean woman is to be immersed in God's Word daily. As Paul writes, "Let the Word of God dwell in you richly" (Col. 3:16). This is simply not possible if you have never read God's Word in its entirety. A deep familiarity with the truth will cause your mental alarm bells to ring when you encounter ideas that deviate from truth. Additionally, becoming aware of some of the traps that authors and speakers fall into is another strategy that will help you spot when content is straying away from God's Word.

STICK TO THE TRUTH, THE WHOLE TRUTH, AND NOTHING BUT THE TRUTH

Some authors share anecdotal accounts from real life that are both touching and wonderfully inspiring. They provide motivation, drive home the relevance of points that have been made, and put flesh and blood and feelings to some of the concepts they have discussed, but when they switch over to teach from God's Word they are less than accurate in handling it. Rather than careful exegesis, too often what is offered instead amounts to superimposing creative retellings of biblical accounts on the actual scriptural texts, which is then coupled with "lessons" that are only derivable from the human retelling, not from the Scripture itself. These makeovers of Scripture tread on dangerous ground in light of the biblical exhortation not to add to God's Word.

Every word of God is flawless; he is a shield to those who take refuge in him. Do not add to his words, or he will rebuke you and prove you a liar. (Prov. 30:5-6)

Do not add to what I command you and do not subtract from it, but keep the commands of the LORD your God that I give you. (Deut. 4:2)

See that you do all I command you; do not add to it or take away from it. (Deut. 12:32)

The fact is, as my friend Karen said, "What God has given to us is sufficient. It doesn't need our help. People will always find reasons to change Scripture, but it's actually quite audacious thinking that we can do a better job than God—make it more understandable, entertaining, less offensive." Recognizing that this is happening can be fairly easy once you train yourself to be alert for certain clue words and phrases. Here are some common "red alert phrases" that often introduce ideas that are from people rather than from God's Word:

- I imagine
- I wouldn't be surprised if
- I wonder if
- It is possible that
- It is likely

- I surmise that
- Perhaps
- Can't you just see
- I have a hunch
- (a biblical character) would have
- I suspect
- My mind goes wild thinking
- Apparently
- Scripture is silent, but likely
- This is just speculation, but

These are just a few of the more common phrases that indicate that a departure from the actual text of Scripture is about to take place. When we read or hear words and phrases like these, our antenna should go up and we should go on red alert. Speculation is not a good foundation on which to build our doctrine or lives.

DEVELOPING DISCERNMENT

Tony was in his twenties when he shared with me that in the middle of a church youth event he found himself murmuring, "Hmm, what's that smell? It's familiar. In fact, I used to be *very* well acquainted with it. Oh yes, it's the smell of the world. What is it doing *here?*" Similarly, a discerning reader or listener is often able to identify the source from which the speaker has been feeding when she hears the content of what he or she is saying. There is a certain flavor that smacks of the world. When psychology, behavioral guidelines, "best practices," and worldly methods of relating interpersonally appear in Christian literature, we need to be on guard. Sometimes they are presented right along with biblical ideas or as if they were solid undisputed truth, even though they have no biblical basis whatsoever. Other times they are not only lacking in biblical basis, but are in direct contradiction with scriptural principles or commands. This is the same for ideas from Eastern Mysticism, evolution, or any number of other philosophical or political worldviews that permeate our culture and steal their way into our thinking and our books. We need to put on our "Berean reading glasses"—you know, the ones with the highest magnification—because when content has not been filtered through the grid of God's Word, it is going to include impurities. The potential for leading others astray is significant and serious. Wrong thinking leads to wrong values, wrong choices, and wrong behavior—sin. "And if anyone causes one of these little ones who believe in me to sin, it would be better for him to be thrown into the sea with a large millstone tied around his neck" (Mark 9:42; see also Matt. 18:6; Luke 17:2).

We have a responsibility to guard ourselves. "Dear children, do not *let* anyone lead you astray" (1 John 3:7, emphasis added). So purpose now that when you come across something that does not seem to align with biblical truth while reading a Christian book, you will stop and check the author's statements. Write the single word "Basis?" in the margin to remind you to go back and examine Scripture for *its* teaching on the subject.

You may ask, "What if I am not really discerning? What if I cannot actually identify the teachings that are unbiblical and the sources from which these wrong teachings are coming? I am beginning to realize that I am in danger of both being led astray myself and of leading others astray by passing on what I have failed to recognize as unbiblical. What can I do about it?"

Allow me to suggest a two-pronged approach. Immerse yourself in God's Word *and* keep your mind free of the influence of the world. Then the presence of the world will stand out for what it is. A mixed diet of simultaneously feeding on the world's fare and on Scripture makes it harder for a person to identify the thinking of the world for what it really is.

Romans 12:2 issues a clarion call to this important task: "Do not conform any longer to the pattern of this world, but be transformed by the renewing of your mind. *Then* you will be able to test and approve what God's will is—his good, pleasing and perfect will" (emphasis added). In this passage, we are told two things: Something we should *not* do and something we *should* do. And both things we are commanded to do require a change. Note the words "transformed" and "renewing." We must also note, however, that this verse comes at a place in Scripture right before the subject of accepting other members in the body of Christ. It is coupled with a reminder of the importance of humility. Even as we evaluate what others write in order to be careful not to be led astray, we must do so with humility, not as self-appointed "lords" over them.

We must also be quick to forgive and to extend grace. We will all make mistakes at some point, even despite our best efforts to accurately handle God's Word. If God's master plan necessitated perfect people, it would have been rendered ineffective from its very inception; it would have ground to a halt before it ever got going. To say we cannot learn from anyone unless their teaching and lives are in perfect order would be foolish. Not only would our own growth be stymied, but we ourselves would not be usable by God to minister to others. Nevertheless, it still falls to us to carefully examine what we allow to influence our beliefs and our actions, and to evaluate carefully all that we hear, read, and watch against Scripture.

I will wrap up this section with a final caution. When you see a pattern of an author repeatedly playing fast and loose with Scripture (again, watch for the clue words mentioned above), you should discard the book altogether. It is dangerous to keep reading a book written by someone who shows little respect for Scripture or limited knowledge of Scripture. And you certainly don't want to recommend such a book to those you are mentoring.

Some suggestions for evaluating books include:

- Look up every reference, and examine the context of quoted references extensively. Make it your practice to always check the biblical text when an author gives a paraphrase of a verse or simply cites a reference without printing the actual verse.
- Be on your guard for certain key words that authors use that indicate they are straying from God's Word (see "red alert phrases" above).
- Make it your practice to check when a scriptural passage is quoted as saying something that you do not remember or have never noticed before. Double check. Is it really there? It could be that you have simply missed it before. Or, it could be that the author is reading something into the text that actually is *not*

there, but would help to make her point or support her opinion if it were.

• Note in the margin when you encounter an unsubstantiated assumption that the author is making but treating as if it were a fact.

• Get into the practice of asking the simple one-word question "Basis?" whenever a claim is made that something is biblical. Determine if there is clear biblical support for it.

IMPLEMENTATION

Book studies can be used in a number of ways. One approach is to read the whole book and then discuss it. Regi Campbell mentors groups of men and distributes required reading lists to all of his mentees. A different book is assigned for each month that the mentorship program runs. After his mentees read the book independently, this is followed up with assignments, application, discussion, and accountability at their monthly meetings.[61]

More typical book studies consist of reading one chapter or lesson per week and answering questions that will be discussed together. If such an approach is used in a mentoring situation, be sure that the element of ongoing accountability is not overlooked. This is not always included in the study questions that some books provide. Equally important is training mentees to be discerning by having them share with you any unbiblical teaching they noticed in their reading.

Ideally, I would recommend that you hold off using book studies with your mentee until after you have been meeting and doing numbers 1–5 and 8–10 of the session components for a while. Then, if there is a good book that covers a topic that addresses an identified area of need in your mentee's life, you could consider doing a book study with her. I highly recommend that you read any book you plan to use ahead of time in order to ascertain if it is indeed a good book. For the study, you would then each read a chapter between sessions, and discuss it when you meet together.

Some books include discussion questions or homework sections to complete. At times, I prefer to ignore these. Instead, my mentee and I

---

[61] Regi Campbell, *Mentor like Jesus* (Nashville, TN: B&H, 2009).

agree that as we read, we will each make notes of memorable content to discuss, noting ideas or sections that speak to us, challenge us, encourage us, or with which we disagree. This then forms the basis of our discussion when we come together. Each week we also try to identify applications from the reading, along with areas where accountability would be helpful. With some mentees I have modified the usual accountability plan so that rather than one way accountability, we each hold the other accountable.

Depending on how closely the study is linked to, dependent on, and permeated with Scripture, a good book study could either take the place of or be in addition to the "Share God's Word" component of a session approach. If you find that appropriate accountability is built into the book study itself through the questions and practical assignments, this could take the place of the accountability component as well.

SOME UNEXPECTED BENEFITS

We touched on some benefits of book studies in the Pros and Cons section. Sometimes a book study will accomplish other unexpected purposes as well, such as making or deepening connections between women that then lead to opportunities for mentoring. I led one a number of years ago that constituted mentoring on one level, which then led to opportunities to mentor on another level. The book study was a small group mentoring arrangement. As God led, I also met with a number of the young women individually at various times. One was Viviana, a sensitive, tenderhearted young lady. God was evidently touching and tugging at her heart and she and I continued to meet one on one to discuss a number of issues after the small group disbanded, and then kept in touch by email and phone calls after she moved away. I was delighted when she returned to our province for a brief stay sometime after this and drove an hour to visit me! The small group book study served as our initial point of connection; our relationship then grew into a continued friendship, which provided opportunities for ongoing prayer for each other, and gave me the opportunity to be a listening ear and a comforting voice in stressful times.

Sometimes speaking sense to a younger woman does not mean calling her *back* to her senses. Sometimes it means reinforcing for her that she *is* on the right track when everyone else around her is telling her that she isn't. Providing that support can help her to *remain* on track in the face of pressure to abandon God's ways. In the absence of such support many younger women will not be able to stand their ground. In Viviana's case, the small group book study served to connect me with a new mentee who not only needed the typical guidance that younger women need but needed this sort of support as well.

Another book study evolved into something more. This time, the initial small group book study developed into a series of several consecutive one-on-one book studies with one of the original members, which ended up spanning a number of years. These began as an older woman helping a younger one; a stronger one, for the moment, helping a weaker one in the midst of an intense struggle. However, before too much time had transpired, the relationship, grounded in God's Word, biblical principles, prayer, and love, blossomed. Under the guidance of God's loving Holy Spirit, the series of book studies very naturally developed into a mutually beneficial accountability partnership, accompanied by a deep and lasting friendship, truly valued by us both. As has happened so often in the story of my life, Rose and I are now miles apart, but still linked together by hearts intertwined and centered on God and His beautiful transforming work in each of our lives. We, too, have been blessed to continue to have quality visits together from time to time, as travel plans allow. Rose recently wrote me these words, "God used you to impact my life in such a significant way, Jo-Anna, (especially through the book studies, gardening, and affirming the role of homemaker) and I pray you'd be encouraged in your ministry to other women."

In one of my earliest interactions with Rose I learned that she was not keen on starting a family any time soon. In fact, when the time did come for her and her husband to have children, the plan was for her to keep right on working; he was going to stay home and care for them. Over the course of many years, God did a complete U-turn on those plans and desires! Rose is now the happy mother of two beautiful children, and a contented and capable homemaker. She is thriving and excelling in her God-given roles. Book studies were one of the means God used to deepen the connection between us, and that relationship played a significant role in getting her back on track in some pretty important areas.

In the end all praise and thanks go to God, who is wise beyond our understanding and the Giver of every good gift. In Viviana's case, the book study was our point of connection, while with Rose it was the means for deepening a connection. While we need to be wise in our choices and alert to the pitfalls, let us not throw out the baby with the bath water when it comes to book studies. God can and does use them to accomplish much good.

Chapter 9

CHOOSING AN APPROACH: SOME CLOSING CONSIDERATIONS

When all is said and done, there are many ways in which the modeling approach and the session approach are similar. The lines between these two approaches are sometimes blurred because quite often one or more components usually associated with one approach are included in the other. Few women will adopt an exclusively session or modeling approach. It is more common to end up with a personalized approach that includes more components from a dominant approach, enhanced with one or two components that more typically fit in the other approach. Thus a mentor who adopts a session approach may choose to include some modeling approach components from time to time and vice versa. As we prepare to move on from the topic of approaches, let me share a few closing considerations about choosing which approach you will use.

MODELING WON'T GET YOU OFF THE HOOK

As you consider whether you will draw more heavily on a modeling approach or a session approach, don't fall into the trap of thinking that the modeling approach will be less demanding. We now know that when we speak of modeling, we are not talking about just living the godliest life we can and hoping younger women will see us and follow the things that we are doing well. In light of the biblical directive for older women to call younger women back

> *"Calling back" requires that mentors are willing to address difficult issues, and correct and call mentees back to lives that glorify God.*

to their senses and get them back on track for following God's purposes and design for their lives, we are going to need to be a great deal more intentional in our approach. We cannot simply "shine our light" and hope for the best. Calling women to live lives that actively glorify God and "talking sense to them" are challenging tasks. There is simply no easy way to do this. So don't choose a modeling approach because you are looking for an easy way out. Modeling won't get you off the hook. The biblical directive remains for older women to *actively* mentor younger women. We cannot expect younger women to become mature followers of Jesus simply through observing our lives.

A biblical modeling approach does not give a mentee the freedom to pick and choose which aspects of your godly example she will embrace and seek to follow. Nor does it mean that the mentor does not verbally address those areas where her mentee is off track. A modeling approach will still require the mentee to be willing to be instructed, guided, and corrected, just as is necessary with a session approach. And it will still require a willingness on the part of the mentor to broach sensitive or difficult issues.

We have also seen that intentional modeling requires planning on the part of the mentor. It will take time to plan what will be modeled and observed, and then additional time to plan for the needed discussions before and after the modeling takes place. Planning for accountability will require time and thought as well. A modeling approach should not be chosen based on the idea that it will be less demanding, take less time, or require less planning than a session approach. Intentional modeling could actually necessitate a greater commitment than sessions in terms of time. However, while time is certainly a significant factor to consider, the effectiveness of an approach cannot be measured by the amount of time invested in it. All this is to say that it cannot be assumed that modeling will be an easier approach or require a lesser investment than sessions.

MENTOR QUALIFICATIONS APPLY
TO BOTH APPROACHES

Another potential misconception to guard against is the idea that the modeling approach is easier because it does not require the mentor to know Scripture well. In reality, to effectively model a godly life we must have a clear picture of what God views as a godly life. More than that, we must be able to explain to our mentees *why* we make certain choices in our lives by taking them back to the Word of God. Ultimately, we want them to learn that it is God's Word that is the authority for our lives— the only rule for our faith and practice. As with the session approach, modeling will require the mentor to know God's standards very well. Biblical literacy is a starting point for any form of biblical mentoring.

On the other hand, a mentor should not think that using a session approach will allow her to live any less of an exemplary life. The apostle Paul tells the Thessalonian believers, "For you yourselves know how you ought to follow our example" (2 Thess. 3:7). This should only be said by one whose life is worth emulating. The same idea is repeated in Philippians 3:17 ("Join with others in following my example, brothers") and Philippians 4:9 ("Whatever you have learned or received or heard from me, or seen in me—put it into practice"). In this case, what the Bible teaches is consistent with conventional wisdom. You have to "walk the walk" as well as "talk the talk" if you want to make a difference. Failing to match life with teaching is, by definition, hypocrisy. Just as biblical literacy is nonnegotiable regardless of which approach to mentoring you adopt, so is having a life that is worthy of imitation (however imperfect we might still be!). Biblical mentors serve as role models. Since both approaches will equally require exemplary living, there is no reason to select an approach based on how you feel you are measuring up to the standard of piety.

Take a look at Paul's approach to bringing the gospel to a new city; it beautifully reflects a biblical approach to mentoring as well:

> *Our gospel came to you not simply with words, but also with power, with the Holy Spirit and with deep conviction. You know how we lived among you for your sake. You became imitators of us and of the Lord; in spite of severe suffering, you welcomed the message with the joy given by the Holy Spirit. And so you became a model to all the believers in Macedonia and Achaia.* (1 Thess. 1:5-7)

In addition to other things, these verses illustrate very well the use of a combination of elements of the two broad approaches to mentoring. Paul and his companions both taught and modeled a life of devotion to God. As godly older women live out as well as teach the power of the gospel to transform lives, they will be examples worth following. As their mentees follow them, they too will become models that others can follow.

Let me conclude this brief chapter with some tips that can be beneficial regardless of the approach that is chosen.

TIPS FOR ALL APPROACHES

- Routine can be helpful for maintaining consistency and predictability so both mentor and mentee know what to expect when they get together.
- Planning or giving an overview of how you will use your time together at the start of your meeting is helpful for some learning styles and personality types.
- Reflection at the close of sessions can be invaluable. As previously mentioned, it cements what has taken place and can inspire ideas for what should happen next.
- Journaling can be a wonderful help in reflection and also provide a record of where you have come from, where you currently are, and

goals that have been accomplished. It can document the growth God has brought in each of you through the process. It can also aid in planning for the future.

Chapter 10

SUBJECTS TO BROACH

WHAT TOPICS DO WE TACKLE?

*Besides the issues in her life, what do I actually talk about with my
mentee? Jesus charged us with teaching disciples to obey everything
He commanded. Where do we begin? Where do we end?*

*If I spend a week or two on each of the seven topics in Titus 2,
won't I run out of material pretty fast? How do I decide what
other topics to cover to help my mentee become "perfect in Christ"?*

Each of these is a valid question. Different people have gone about
answering them in different ways. Some answers are more firmly
grounded in Scripture, and others more loosely so. Several use Scripture
as a starting point, only to quickly leap away from that foundation.

Scripture, though, should never be a springboard that allows us to launch into our own "wisdom." Scripture should be what guides us. It alone can take us and our mentees to a place where we are "complete, equipped for every good work" (2 Tim. 3:17, NIV 2011).

GOALS AND CURRICULUM

God has made it very clear that all believers should be increasing in Christlikeness. This is our broad overarching goal. Our mentoring should work towards accomplishing this goal, keeping in mind that there will be some unique expressions of Christlikeness for women in general (as distinct from men), and for younger women in particular. In the process of working towards this Christlikeness, or godliness, there are many specifics that young women will need to be taught. Mentors may have a master list of topics that they want to discuss with their mentees and study from Scripture together, as well as activities they wish to do with their mentees for the purpose of training them to be godly.

There are some subjects every believer needs to study and work on. There are others that will be of particular importance for a specific woman because of her personality, history, interests, needs, life circumstances, gifts, weaknesses, or strengths. A new mentor may want to begin with the basics that everyone needs to master and then branch out into other areas as she gains confidence and familiarity with her mentee and her needs, and finds her own niche in mentoring.

We are well aware that as mentees face various challenges in their lives these will prompt a number of questions for which they will be seeking answers. Questions may also stem from life experiences, their reading of Scripture, relational issues, or other matters. As mentors help mentees to navigate these issues in scriptural ways, they will find themselves addressing a variety of topics. The subjects that present themselves may be included among those that are prescribed in Scripture, or they may be in addition to them. The mentor's goal is to guide her mentee to get her back on track, so that she lives in a way that is pleasing to God and brings glory to His name. Keeping this goal in mind will be very helpful for the mentor as she makes decisions about which topics to address and how much priority each should receive in terms of time and focus. So, how do you as a mentor create a working list of subjects to broach with your mentee?

THE SHORT LIST?

One approach taken by many has been to address the seven topics found in Titus 2 exclusively. This list has been the subject of numerous books, and many women have used these as either a springboard for their mentoring programs or the sum total of what is taught to mentees. There are four considerations related to the short list in Titus 2 to which we should give some thought.

Mentoring is More than Titus 2

First, although the seven topics of Titus 2:4-5 are of special importance for women, we should not read this passage to imply that these topics are to be the sole emphasis for mentoring younger women. Instead, they represent specific areas of character construction that must be built on the broader foundation of discipleship that is outlined throughout the New Testament. Remember, followers of Jesus are called to make disciples and teach them "to obey everything [He] commanded" (Matt. 28:20), with the goal being to present each one "perfect in Christ" (Col. 1:28). As you consider what topics to broach with your mentee, it is critical to keep these more foundational goals of what it means to be a follower of Jesus firmly in view.

Advance Preparation for Mentors

Second, once one has understood the nature of the role given to older women, the scope of the task, and the outcome desired by God, it becomes readily apparent that many older women are not presently up for the task. Some lack equipping. Others need to be "*sophronizo*-ed" themselves. Whether they have been influenced by their culture or their flesh, many older women have clearly gotten off track. Others simply lack an understanding of Scripture and of what God through Paul's letter to Titus is calling them to be and to do. Being off track themselves makes it impossible for them to help the younger women to get back on track. Even worse, if older women who are off track write resources based on erroneous foundations, they become culpable of actually *directing* others off track as well.

Before older women attempt to teach others how to get on track, they need to be on track themselves. This is what church leaders (like Titus) should be teaching older women, but it is also something you can work hard at yourself. The description in Titus 2 is both commanded for older women and it is attainable. Of course, none of us is perfect, but downplaying the importance of God's Word and presuming to train other mentors or even our own mentees without first giving serious attention to ensuring we ourselves are on track is dangerous and contrary to Scripture. Older women must first be taught to be godly in all the ways that Paul describes in Titus 2:3, "in order that" they may call younger women back to their senses (Titus 2:4). The bottom line is, until a woman is on track herself with her life marked by devotion to God and piety, she is not qualified to guide others back on track. Attempting to serve as a mentor of younger women when you are unprepared or unqualified is dangerous for you as well as for the mentee (Matt. 18:6; Mark 9:42; Luke 17:1-2).

Advance Preparation for Mentees
A third related issue is the question of how biblical mentoring following Titus 2 relates to mentees who are single or do not have children. Since three of the items in the short list in Titus 2 address relationships with husbands and children, some may ask, "Should we talk about loving husbands with a mentee who is not married? Or loving children with one who is not yet a mother?" Is it appropriate to call a mentee back to a standard that seemingly does not apply to her? I believe that it is. In reality, this is a major part of all discipleship. For example, a youth ministry that is biblical will not simply be teaching youth how to be godly youth; it will be teaching them how to be godly adults. A solid children's ministry will not simply teach children how to be godly children; it will train them how to live in a godly manner at every stage of their lives. Taking a more comprehensive and proactive approach will mean broaching topics that cover not just current experiences, but anticipated ones. As you know, many truths are not learned overnight

or in a single two-hour session. If you wait until your mentee is dating, engaged, pregnant, or a new mother, it is quite possible that you will end up short-changing her. You see, sometimes it takes the cement a while to set. Allow me to explain.

When our oldest son was 11 or 12 years old, my good friend Eileen, whose son was a year older, paid us a visit. She was reading a book about dating. It was premature for her own son as well, but she explained to me that she wanted to read it now in order to be prepared ahead of time for the issue. I followed suit. It turned out to be an excellent plan. I read the book. My sons and husband did not. This spared them from allowing certain images and activities described in the book into their minds. Marty and I simply discussed some of the pertinent principles contained in its pages, and then from time to time I would initiate a conversation with our children in which I would share our views on the topic of dating and marriage and the values we wanted to instill in them to guard and guide their future relationships. Our young children all very naturally accepted this, and internalized these values and principles as their own. By the time they hit puberty and the hormones came to glorious, vibrant life, that wall of protection had been built. And the cement had set. Because it had been done ahead of time, we experienced no turbulence whatsoever. Had we waited until the hormones were raging to begin to introduce the restraining wall, it might not have held. The wet cement could easily have given way, leaving behind only destruction rather than a strong solid fence of protection.

Not everyone will get married in the end, and not every married mentee will go on to become a mother, but being prepared to love a husband and child still remains valuable and well worth knowing. At the time this was written, well known speaker and author Nancy DeMoss Wolgemuth had never been married or experienced motherhood, but using biblical principles she had nonetheless been an excellent counselor of wives and mothers, and had been used by God to bless, inspire, challenge, and correct thousands. I'm glad she was trained in all the Titus 2 principles, and not just the ones that seemed to apply to her personally!

Take God's Word at Face Value

This brings us very naturally to the question that the last paragraph may have raised for some. What about single mentors and those without children. Can they still mentor younger women given what Titus 2 says? As we address this issue, we have a wonderful opportunity to think about how Scripture rather than experience must serve as our foundation. We want to avoid a trap that is so common today: "Well, so-and-so did it and God blessed her; so it must be okay." The fact that Nancy DeMoss Wolgemuth effectively mentored countless married women and mothers when she herself was neither does not validate the practice, in and of itself. We are all well aware that God spoke a striking message through Balaam's donkey (Num. 22:21-34), but we don't see the New Testament approving donkeys for elders and preachers, now do we? The bottom line must remain, "What does Scripture say?"

What are the qualifications for a mentor? What makes an older woman equipped to *sophronizo* younger women? These are not rhetorical questions. This is a test. We have already talked about this. She is to be godly, pious, devout; she is to be reverent in the way she lives. Now it's application time. Can a single woman be pious? Can those without children be devout? Can they teach what is good, exhibit control of their speech, refrain from addictions, and in all other ways demonstrate the power of God to transform lives? I hope you answered with a resounding "Yes!" If we are going to allow Scripture to be our standard, then we need to commit to taking it at face value and obeying it and leaving the results and the questions to God.

Are you pious? Are you devout? Do the other descriptions in Titus 2 match your character? Then you meet the qualifications for mentoring younger women regardless of whether you are single or married, childless or the mother of ten children. The world says that you need to have experienced marriage and children to mentor those in those situations— and that certainly can be helpful; but God says you need to have been molded into a woman of God to mentor younger women. God can use you. He wants to use you. He has called you, devoted older woman, to retrain the younger women He has placed in your life. Do not shrink back. Forge ahead in dependence on Him.

WESLEY'S TRIED AND TRUE LIST

Over 200 years ago, in his sermon, "On the Education of Children," John Wesley, founder of Methodism, proposed the idea of diseases "natural to every human soul" as a framework for addressing child training.[62] He began by recognizing that Scripture points to a number of sins to which all humans are especially predisposed. His "curriculum" set out to address and propose a remedy for each one that he identified. This approach resonated with me from the

---

WESLEY'S LIST

1. Atheism
2. Pride
3. Love of the world
4. Anger
5. Deviation from truth
6. Unjust speech/actions

---

moment I first encountered it. Although my children were still living at home at that time, they were no longer young. Nevertheless, besides realizing some mistakes I had made in my early child rearing years, I also found a number of ideas that it was not too late to incorporate. I have found this approach to be helpful for mentoring as well. The idea of seeing humans as being marred or diseased and in need of remedy fits very well with the idea of calling people back to a standard (*sophronizo*). As humans, we are often off track and in need of correction and instruction. The idea of "diseases of one's nature," or besetting sins to which we are predisposed, also dovetails especially well with the personalized aspect of mentoring. As mentors grow in discernment and experience, they are often able to identify manifestations of this spiritual disease as a mentee shares her life issues. This can be an important part of setting the course and determining

The idea of "diseases of one's nature" is biblical, and dovetails especially well with the remedial nature of sophronizo

which topics to teach on and discuss together. We older women could really benefit from Wesley's wise approach as we seek to call younger

---

[62] John Wesley, *On the Education of Children*, Sermon 95. Online: www.umcmission. org/Find-Resources/John-Wesley-Sermons/Sermon-95-On-the-Education-of-Children. Accessed June 19, 2015.

women to get back on track. Let's look a bit more closely at what he has to say.

Atheism is the first foundational disease Wesley addresses. The application for grown young women will be different than those Wesley proposed for infants and toddlers, but the truths are universal. When self-worship and self-will are rooted out of a young woman's life and replaced with worship of God and submission to His will, she will find it far easier to love her husband and children and submit to the authorities that have been ordained and placed in her life by God.

Pride manifests itself in myriads of ways, making it not a matter of whether your mentee will suffer from this disease, but rather of determining the ways in which her pride is harming her. Your role, even as you work to rid yourself of your own pride, will be to help her recognize how pride has taken root in her and discover how you can best help her to find the healing and victory over it that she needs.

Love of the world is the next disease "natural to every human soul" that Wesley mentions. Anger, deviation from the truth, and the tendency to speak or act contrary to justice round out his list.

In our cultural milieu we like to be non-confrontational and "positive." We find it more acceptable to simply say we will study God's existence, rather than saying we need to address the disease of atheism. We prefer to teach on humility, truth, and loving God with all our hearts, rather than addressing pride, deception, and love of the world. However, the calling back aspect of *sophronizo* requires more than just a few "positive" talks. John Wesley's approach captures the essence of this, first identifying the problems and then proposing a remedy for each.

A "LIFE EXPERIENCE" LIST

Another way of approaching mentoring is using a working list that is based on life experiences. Evelyn Christensen speaks of the importance of mentoring out of our own experiences *and* about the need to meet people where they are at. "People would say to me, 'Evelyn, don't start teaching where *you* are now. Please start teaching where *we* are now, where you were then.' I had to learn that, to go back to where they are.

That's extremely important."[63] In light of this, a life experience list would be based on the mentor's life, but be chosen in light of the mentee's current circumstances and stage of life.

Regi Campbell also advocates that mentors share with their mentees out of what God has taught them. Emphasizing topical Scripture memory, he recommends teaching mentees the Scriptures God has strategically used in our lives.[64] Such an approach allows the mentor to speak with authenticity. Given the temptation to overwhelm a young mentee with years of lessons you have learned all at once, however, Campbell also cautions, "Jesus didn't teach on every verse He knew. He met needs."[65]

Campbell is working with a different model than the call to older women found in Titus 2. Nevertheless, there is value in considering the subjects he chooses to cover, which correspond to Scripture verses he requires his mentees to memorize:

CAMPBELL'S LIST

Priorities	Faith
Purpose	Teaching Your Children
Fruit	Talk
Fear	Work
Humility and Gentleness	Motives
Peace	Thought Life
Decision Making	Time
Contentment	Honor
Spiritual Warfare	Self-denial
Decisiveness	Selflessness
Wisdom	Prayer
Light	

Even from the few lists we've considered above, it will be easy to see that each person could readily come up with their own list, and that while these lists would likely have many parallels, each would be unique.

---

[63] Evelyn Christenson, "Grace for Aging." Online: www.reviveourhearts.com/radio/revive-our-hearts/grace-aging/. Accessed June 17, 2013, italics added.

[64] Campbell, *Mentor Like Jesus*, 87.

[65] Ibid., 92.

In our Cypress Hills Ministries Women Mentoring Women workshops, participants are asked to begin creating their own initial lists of subjects for broaching with mentees. More than once, after the workshop I have been asked for a copy of my list...as well as a blueprint of the approach I use. Participants sometimes want a step-by-step guide of what to do. I do have a list of subjects to broach with mentees, and I am going to share it with you. But before doing so, there is one more important matter we need to discuss. You see, part of the reason that lists can be so diverse is that each of our lists will flow out of our own thinking and our own personal philosophy; and even though we are all part of the same Body of Christ, these can be very different. If you are one who is asking, "Once we get past jotting down the most basic topics, how do we go about creating the rest of our lists?" and, "Are there any guidelines that can help us stay grounded and focus on what is most needed and most important for our mentee?", then you will want to pay close attention to the next chapter. In fact, I invite you to take some extended time to prepare your heart before reading it. Ask God to give you an open mind, a teachable spirit, and the patience to consider it all before drawing your conclusions. Ask our Guide and Teacher, the Holy Spirit, to lead you into all truth. And then, with your Bible in hand to check up on me, read on.

Chapter 11

PHILOSOPHY MATTERS

Philosophy matters. Yes, the play on words is intended; no, you are not missing a punch line. No humor is intended. Our philosophy is a serious matter. It impacts how we approach all we do and all that we experience in this life. It will impact which topics you choose to address with your mentee, and it will determine *how you choose to address them.* As you have read the pages of this book, you have been immersed in my philosophy. I hope you have seen a strong discipleship focus, motivated by God's glory, and firmly grounded in God's Word. There are many other philosophies, however.

DISCIPLESHIP OR ENTERTAINMENT?
It was then that God's Holy Spirit convicted me. It was as clear as the water in a mountain stream. I knew exactly what He was talking about and why He was saying it. And because it was so unmistakable, I have not forgotten it. In

His love, He has used the guidance I received through this experience in my life ever since, and it has helped to keep me on track on the straight and narrow, directing me away from the allure of the broad way.

My third grade class had spent the last several days trying their hardest to convince the other third grade classes that leprechauns were real—along with anyone else in the whole K–8 school who would listen. I had done a convincing job in my efforts to inspire art and language arts projects! Just a few months earlier, however, I had conspicuously avoided the buzz of excitement that accompanied the arrival of The Polar Express, *the then-new creative Christmas story by Chris Van Allsburd that almost every other teacher was finding a way to incorporate into her room. I had avoided that train because I hadn't wanted anything to compete with the truth of the real story, the true miracle of Christmas. Looking back on the March that followed, I'm not sure why it took God's voice for me to recognize the large "H" for hypocrite written across my chest as I poured all my imaginative energies into creating the mirage that leprechauns were visiting our classroom each night. I am so grateful He intervened. When my students discovered I had been a leprechaun myself, tricking them, would they then doubt all the truths of God's story I had already shared and those I still hoped to share with them? As soon as I saw this, I made my decision. From that point on I would use the gift of creativity that God gave me* for His glory.

When Saint Patrick's Day rolled around the next time, I taught *about* the fun idea of leprechauns, but my *focus* was different. I introduced my class to the historical person whose day we celebrate. I taught about facts and legends. We talked about the country of Ireland, my half-Irish grandmother, Irish potatoes, and we made stone soup together. On Valentine's Day, we took a similar approach, learning about the legends surrounding the Christian physician who was martyred for his faith and for his willingness to perform weddings. We focused on what real love means. We talked about romantic love and the commitment of a husband and a wife.

Later, when I taught Pre-Kindergarten, each year we held a wedding in our room, celebrating the marriage of the letters Q and U, who "always stick together," and playing the video of my own wedding. Along the way, learning terms like *groomsmen, maid of honor,* and *flower girl* helped these little ones, many of whose parents were not married—meet the Pre-K objectives of language development. Local florists donated flowers, children donned their Sunday best, and parent helpers provided a lovely reception for the special occasion each year. Once we even had a real preacher, a dear family friend with a propensity for acting and a twinkle in his eye, come and perform the marriage ceremony of Q and U!

Creativity is a gift from God. Creativity run amuck can be a huge obstacle to God's work. It is often at cross purposes with it. However, the idea that creativity could compete with God for glory and easily robs Him of it is seldom recognized. We like to have our cake and eat it too. Surely God is pleased with the big show! After all, we have put so much work into it, and people really seemed to enjoy it. After all, God was the One who made me creative to begin with. Surely He wants me to use my talents!

> *Creativity is a gift from God. But creativity run amuck can actually be an obstacle to God's work.*

As we approach the entertainment-discipleship choice, many questions may surface:

What is an entertainment model?
What is a discipleship model?
Why are people drawn to one or the other?
What are the strengths of each?
What are the dangers?
How can I tell where what I am doing fits in?
How can I identify where I may need to make changes in my thinking, programming, or planning?

And perhaps the most important question of all:

What did Jesus do?

The entertainment model is a particularly popular one, and often ends up competing with a discipleship-based philosophy. It emphasizes fun, and often uses what may be identified as worldly pleasure to try to make Christianity "attractive." It is often evidenced by a focus on events, the desire to draw crowds, and the methods used to draw them. In youth settings these may include games, recreational activities, contests, food and snacks, outings, or bringing in a wide range of entertainment. In churches it is often seen in "The Big Show," where the emphasis is on performance, staging, the latest technology, emotional appeal, humor, catchy programs, flashy media, and food. The same approach is sometimes present in mentoring programs as well.

One plan incorporates special luncheons each of the six weeks that the women meet to learn how to cook and discuss the topics in Titus 2. The cooking lesson happens largely by observing demonstrations and taking notes. Learning how to cook is very valuable. And six of the topics listed in Titus 2 are discussed. I found, in fact, many commendable features in this program. However, I would identify it as an entertainment model rather than a discipleship one for a number of reasons. These include the short time taken on the whole program (seven weeks), the disproportionate time spent on the cooking each week, the choice of menu items (and the cost of the program), and the overt emphasis on pampering the women who participate.[66] Calling younger women back to their senses involves teaching them to obey everything Jesus commanded, and that includes the call to deny themselves, take up their cross, and follow Jesus. This does not mesh very well with programs that pamper them!

By contrast, speaking of the importance of discipleship, Anne Ortlund says, "This is how you build a strong church from the inside out. Your growth does not come from onlookers being attracted to a superstar in the pulpit until a more scintillating star arrives at a church down the street. You start discipling an intimate few of your eager ones, who will each do the same the next year. And without your hardly knowing what has happened, you will soon have dozens of "pastors" in

---

[66] "There is much conversation and laughter. The women are enjoying a day out, one made especially for them. They are welcomed, loved and pampered for two-and-a-half or more hours for six weeks. I am always impressed with how lovely the women look. For them, it is almost like going to a party." Huizenga, *Apples of Gold*, 11.

your church; they'll be pastoring each other."[67] These two approaches highlight for us a significant difference in philosophy.

One of the apparent "strengths" of the entertainment model is in its appeal to the flesh: Who doesn't want to eat gourmet food? If I am honest, my first thought when I am invited for a gourmet meal is to mentally select what I will wear! I like cooking gourmet meals, and I like eating them; and it's a double treat when someone else has done the work to prepare it! Scripture records a lot of good eating going on. And God is preparing the banquet to end all banquets for us (Rev. 19:9). Wow! But when we look at the whole counsel of God's Word, we see that although there will be times for celebrating in the here and now as well as in eternity, during this present time our *focus* is to be on God's work. There is a time for work and a time for celebration. Jesus tells us to work now while we can, as the day is coming when we will no longer have that opportunity (John 9:4; 4:34; 17:14). Time is short. There is much to do. Of course there are times when we can and should celebrate, but if the *focus* of our lives is one big party rather than doing the work that God has set before us, we are living in disobedience.

Follow Me

Disobedience is a strong word, especially from one who loves a good party, which I do. How can I call this focus *disobedience*? Well, we have been clearly told to follow Jesus. I read Jesus' words in the last chapter of John again in my devotional time this morning. Peter had been told a difficult thing. He was going die a painful death and he needed to follow Jesus' example in this—dying in such a way that God would receive glory from it. You and I don't have specifics about the way we will die. But we, like Peter, need to purpose to glorify God by both living well and dying well. The way we live and the way we mentor is our current focus. Jesus lived a life of work and service that was focused on God's glory and on His assignment from God, the completion of which would bring God that glory. If we are following Jesus, we will be so set on completing the assignment given to us by God that we will daily do our

---

[67] Anne Ortlund, "Chapter Eight, Discipling: Catch the Vision" in *Heart to Heart with Pastor's Wives*, ed. Lynne Dugan (Ventura, CA.: Regal, 1994), 91.

best to ensure that not one of the good works God planned in advance for us to do is left undone. We will not be sidetracked.

When Jesus told Peter to follow Him, He then had to deal with a question that is typical of you and me as well: "But Jesus, what about so and so?" Jesus' answer amounts to this: Whether or not anyone else is following Him has no bearing at all on His requirement that *I* follow Him. What Jesus may or may not ask others to do is irrelevant. Like Peter, I must follow the path marked out for me (John 21:22). Jesus came, He lived, He died, and He lives again. He showed me the way to live and to die. I do not have to guess how to follow Him; He has already shown me. As Jerry Bridges points out, the question is not "What *would* Jesus do?" as if it were left up to us to imagine the answer, but rather, "What *did* Jesus do?" He did come and He did show us.[68] Many philosophies of ministry exist. My task, and yours, is to examine Scripture to see the example Jesus left for us in life and in ministry, and to follow Him.

What Jesus Did
It should not surprise us to learn that Jesus had a philosophy of ministry too. When we looked at mentoring approaches, we saw Jesus using teaching and modeling and ministering together to make disciples. We know that we who are His disciples are commanded to make more disciples. Jesus lived in a time and place that was every bit as rich in culture as our society today. There were talented musicians and dancers, eloquent speakers, philosophical debates, impressive theatrical productions, amphitheaters, and sports fanaticism that rivals our culture today. Yet we do not see Jesus training a dance troupe or drama team to accompany Him on His mission trips. He did not draw a crowd by doing impersonations or stand-up comedy routines. He was brilliant. He could have had people roaring with laughter, and then pinned them with a closing line or two that cut them to the core with conviction. But He didn't. He did use allegory and parables. He certainly drew crowds with His miracles, including feeding huge groups of people with next to

---

[68] Jerry Bridges, foreword to *Walking Like Jesus Did: Studies in the Character of Christ* by Larry McCall (Winona Lake, IN: BMH, 2005), iv.

nothing. They came because He healed people and showed His power over demons. Jesus did all these things, but mostly He taught them. He proclaimed the kingdom of God and urged them to repent of their sins, believe He was the Messiah, and be saved. He knew some were just there for the food, or to see a miracle, but this did not prevent Him from multiplying the bread or raising the dead. His purpose for doing these things was never to entertain. Jesus' actions and teachings were always focused on meeting real needs. And what He chose to do was always determined by a clear goal. He wanted to complete the work His Father had given Him to do. This was His sole measure of success. This was what satisfied our Lord.

> *"My food," said Jesus, "is to do the will of him who sent me and to finish his work. Do you not say, 'Four months more and then the harvest'? I tell you, open your eyes and look at the fields! They are ripe for harvest. Even now the reaper draws his wages, even now he harvests the crop for eternal life, so that the sower and the reaper may be glad together. Thus the saying 'One sows and another reaps' is true. I sent you to reap what you have not worked for. Others have done the hard work, and you have reaped the benefits of their labor."* (John 4:34-38)

Scripture does not always tell us why Jesus did certain things. There will be differences of opinion as to why Jesus did what He did and did not do what He did not do. Some will want to follow His methods as closely as possible, while some will feel that the broad use of recreation, entertainment, and the arts are perfectly fine and greatly enhance their productivity or fruitfulness. Is this a gray area where we are free to make our own choice, or do any other Scriptures shed light on this issue?

What Scripture Teaches
The apostle Paul gives us some great insight when he writes about his own deliberate choice not to use impressive speech:

For Christ did not send me to baptize, but to preach the gospel—
not with words of human wisdom, lest the cross of Christ be
emptied of its power. *For the message of the cross is foolishness
to those who are perishing, but to us who are being saved it is
the power of God. For it is written: "I will destroy the wisdom of
the wise; the intelligence of the intelligent I will frustrate." Where
is the wise man? Where is the scholar? Where is the philosopher
of this age? Has not God made foolish the wisdom of the world?
For since in the wisdom of God the world through its wisdom did
not know him, God was pleased through the foolishness of what
was preached to save those who believe. Jews demand miraculous
signs and Greeks look for wisdom, but we preach Christ crucified:
a stumbling block to Jews and foolishness to Gentiles, but to those
whom God has called, both Jews and Greeks, Christ the power of
God and the wisdom of God. For the foolishness of God is wiser
than man's wisdom, and the weakness of God is stronger than man's
strength. Brothers, think of what you were when you were called.
Not many of you were wise by human standards; not many were
influential; not many were of noble birth. But God chose the foolish
things of the world to shame the wise; God chose the weak things
of the world to shame the strong. He chose the lowly things of this
world and the despised things—and the things that are not—to
nullify the things that are, so that no one may boast before him.* (1
Cor. 1:17-29, emphasis added.)

As humans we are riddled with pride. We are easily caught up in
our musical talents, our artistic abilities, our creative ideas, and our
ability to draw a crowd. When we succeed and appeal to the masses,
we face the temptation of boasting of our accomplishments. We are
prone to take credit for ourselves. We are tempted to rob God of His
glory. We can end up receiving glory from others and not directing it
back to God and giving Him full credit for what He has accomplished
through us, His servants. "What do you have that you did not receive?
If then you received it, why do you boast as if you did not receive it?"
(1 Cor. 4:7).

First Corinthians 1:17 is sobering. *We can actually rob the gospel of its power by our human wisdom and philosophies.* Although it may impress others, using the world's ways can actually render the gospel message ineffective. This happens when our approach to ministry does not flow out of a transformed mind, but rather reflects a mind that trusts in the ways of the world rather than the power of God. If we mimic the world in how we draw a crowd, what does that communicate about our message? If we are going to attempt to convince that crowd that God is powerful, would it not increase the effectiveness of our testimony if our methods were consistent with our message? If we use the love of pleasure to draw people in, how can we then, once they are in, turn around and ask them to deny themselves? Is there a big "H" for hypocrite lurking in there somewhere?

What are we thinking by trying to "draw people to God" by feeding their fleshly desires? The love of pleasure is clearly contrasted with the love of God in Scripture (2 Tim. 3:4), and love of self is contrasted with love of God and love of others.[69] First John 2:15-17 also tells us that it is impossible to love both the world and God: "Do not love the world or anything in the world. If anyone loves the world, the love of the Father is not in him. For everything in the world—the cravings of sinful man, the lust of his eyes and the boasting of what he has and does—comes not from the Father but from the world." Verse 17 concludes, "The world and its desires pass away, but the man who does the will of God lives forever."

Guard Your Focus, Stay on Target

So, how does our awareness of these teachings in Scripture and the way that Jesus lived shape how we make our decisions about life and ministry? How does it affect how we will approach mentoring and what topics we will cover? How do we determine what is good and right, or how much pleasure is too much? For me, a lot comes down to goals and motives. Is this truly being done to bring glory to God? Is it furthering

---

[69] "People will be lovers of themselves" (2 Tim. 3:2) is in a list of sins, and contrasts with the often repeated commands to love God and love others (see Gal. 5:14; James 2:8; Lev. 19:18; Deut. 6:5; 10:12; 11:13).

His kingdom? Am I giving God the credit before others, both saved and lost, for what I am doing or celebrating?

In addition to examining our goals and motives, we often also have to navigate the influence of others. Perhaps you have come across some of the wide variety of "fun activities" advocated under the topic of loving children and husbands in some mentoring models: socials and recreational events, weekly mother-daughter dates, regular overnight hotel trips, shopping trips, and many similar

> *Denying ourselves generally steers us a totally different direction than entertaining ourselves.*

activities. Perhaps, if you were not engaging in these activities, you wondered if you were not loving your family as well as you should be. Perhaps you secretly wished your budget would *allow* you to better love your family this way. Pampering and recreational activities, however, do not readily mesh with the descriptions of love we find in Scripture. And they are certainly not easily reconciled with Christ's call to deny one's self. It is, therefore, hard to see how a focus on such things accomplishes the goals of mentoring.

Thirty years of marriage is truly a gift from God! Friendship and fellowship over a meal is a gift from God too. But when my family, friends, church leaders, or others encourage me to make it my practice to spend excessive time and money (resources entrusted to me by God) on my own pleasures, then I need to step back for a moment. I need to distance myself enough to evaluate whether they are leading me to become more like Jesus, or less like Him. Jesus denied Himself and kept His focus on serving others. He did not allow Himself to be sidetracked by anyone who attempted to lead Him away from the cross. The cross, painful as it would be, was His ultimate job assignment, His goal. When Peter tried to deter Him, He rebuked him as a pawn of the evil one, and called for those who follow Him to deny themselves.[70] Denying ourselves will generally steer us in a totally different direction than entertaining ourselves. When the Pharisees tried to "protect" Him from the cross, Jesus deftly sidestepped the temptation, refocused on the goal,

[70] See Matthew 16:21-27.

and kept on going.[71] If our goal is to follow Jesus, we will do likewise. We will keep our sights fixed on the goal laid out before us, and not allow ourselves to be sidetracked. I am not speaking about the occasional special meal or celebration (an anniversary, for example, is something to celebrate!), but I am speaking of escaping a lifestyle of self-indulgence.

The arts have been around since the beginning (Gen. 4:21), and we see in Scripture how they can be used for God's glory (Exod. 26, 28, 35). But the conception that recreation and entertainment are every person's right, and the huge amounts of time and money invested in them today, is a more recent phenomenon. Perhaps something pivotal occurred with the invention of the motion picture camera. Surely Thomas Edison could not have imagined what his invention would eventually lead to! Today our city's budget is so heavily weighted towards providing recreation and arts that it is astounding. It is no longer enough to manage the city's infrastructure and provide services; providing for entertainment is seen as a governmental duty, and participating in recreation as every citizen's right. But we belong to another kingdom. We must keep this firmly in mind despite the pull of our own flesh, the swirling vortex of our culture, and any schemes the evil one may throw our way to lure us off track.

Points of Agreement

Whatever our thoughts on the entertainment model, we should all be able to agree that we are to avoid self-indulgence ourselves and avoid promoting it for others. We can also agree that we must keep the goal of making disciples front and center. We must seek to always maintain a high view of Scripture and an unwillingness to depart from it, either by adding to it or subtracting from it. We must remember that *the gospel* is the power of God for salvation. It is *in Christ* that all the treasures of wisdom and knowledge are hidden (Col. 2:3). *He* is the pearl of great value, not the wrapping that we may want to package Him up in.

When all the trappings and embellishments are stripped away—the "words of human wisdom" that Paul speaks of in 1 Corinthians 1—we will then be left with the simple power of the gospel, and a focus on

---

[71] When Jesus says, "I will reach my goal" in Luke 13:31-33, He is referring to His death on the cross.

discipleship and being about God's business. And God will be the One Who receives *all* the glory.

He was already old. He wore T-shirts and jeans and drove a pickup truck. Each week he picked up the boys for a Bible study and dropped them home afterwards. There were no "fun" activities. Other than occasional weekend retreats at his cabin, they never did a social event.

Bob Ennen was the most influential Christian in my husband's life.

Some years ago his obituary appeared in the paper in his hometown, which we had long since left, and my mother-in-law clipped it out for us. It was simple. Just like his life had been.

Many years after my husband was taught by Bob, he had his first and only opportunity to counsel at a Christian youth camp. He was already the father of our three children at the time. During the week he was there, he didn't participate with the campers in many of the scheduled activities. In fact, he didn't do any of the things that people say you have to do to build a relationship with youth or "win the right" to speak to them about spiritual things. He merely taught them from the Word in the evenings, showing them how the Scriptures spoke to the issues in their lives, and giving them an opportunity to ask about things that were on their hearts. And boy, did they open up! Most of them had been heavily involved in youth group for years, but seemed to have never had a chance to ask a spiritual leader for help with the challenges they were facing or answers to the questions they had about God and life as a Christian. In fact, more than once the boys under his care begged him to stay back in the cabin with them to teach them from God's Word, even though it meant missing their turns at canoeing or archery, or the climbing wall or zip line.

When he came home, he taught us all the new camp and worship songs he had learned, which we enjoyed for years to come. I have vivid memories of our three little children singing with wild abandon, often dancing about, and occasionally even jumping from couch to couch or bed to bed in their elation as they sang them. Perhaps the campers retained their memories of that week too—and the times they chose to learn about God's truths in their cabin rather than participate in the many exciting activities that had been open to them.

I still thank God for Bob Ennen. Through his influence on my husband, Bob's legacy continues to this day. "A student is not above his teacher, but everyone who is fully trained will be like his teacher" (Luke 6:40).

SCRIPTURE-BASED OR NEEDS-BASED?

A second major choice that you will have to make as you determine your philosophy of ministry is between a Scripture-driven and a needs-driven approach. The latter has become very popular, making it very easy to be pulled into it almost without being aware that you have made a choice. Many who in practice actually advocate a needs-driven model will nonetheless begin by claiming to be Scripture-based.[72] Certainly we should be aware of the needs of those to whom we minister, but these needs are far better identified by the One who is best able to do so, rather than by the individuals themselves. The fact that humanity is plagued by both selfishness and self-deception naturally affects our ability to identify and accurately assess our own genuine needs. It is very easy to refer to our *wants* as needs. It is easy to call our personal preferences or what would make life convenient for us our needs.

Mentoring ministries, women's ministries, and even whole church ministries are sometimes built on the foundation of "felt needs" and surveys. "What do congregants think they need?" "What is most important to our women?" Surveying felt needs seems like a sensitive and caring route to take, and there are certainly appropriate times for survey use, but when it comes to identifying real needs for the purpose of setting the direction and focus of a ministry or a mentoring partnership, God's Word provides the surer foundation. He is the One who knows all our real needs, has identified them for us, and will direct us how to meet them. Surveys can be skewed by poorly worded questions, and the results are usually open to interpretation. Even more problematic, they

---

[72] Edwards and Neumann, *Organic Mentoring*. See also Tricia Scribner and Edna Ellison, *Woman to Woman: Preparing Yourself to Mentor* (Birmingham: New Hope, 2011). By contrast, the survey use recommended by Vicky Kraft and Gwynne Johnson in *Women Mentoring Women: Ways to Start, Maintain and Expand a Women's Ministry* (Chicago: Moody, 2003) is generally supportive of a Scripture-based approach to women's ministry.

usually draw on information and opinions solicited from the spiritually immature as well as the spiritually mature. By contrast, "all Scripture is God-breathed and profitable for teaching, rebuking, correcting and training in righteousness, so that the man of God may be thoroughly equipped for every good work" (2 Tim. 3:16-17). I am not saying here that surveys should never be used. One appropriate and beneficial use of surveys would be to help reveal broadly how women in a particular church need to be called back to their senses.

Let me illustrate how easy it is to slip into elevating needs-based surveys (and one's own ideas) above God's clear Word. Look at how one book on mentoring portrays the requirements found in Scripture for a mentor, and how the authors made their own decision regarding what qualifies an older woman for this role. This discussion comes under the heading "Competing with the Titus 2 Woman":

> One reason women feel inadequate to mentor is that they compare themselves with an imaginary, heroic Christian woman who leaps tall buildings in a single bound and also teaches a women's Bible study. Titus 2:3 is the Scripture most often used as a guideline for mentoring. Read Titus 2:3. *How do you feel* after reading this passage?[73]

After some blank lines, the authors continue:

> If you said, "Whew! What a job description, and where's the back door?" join the ranks. The requirements of Titus 2:3 can be rather intimidating. I have a bone to pick with the writer of this verse. First, I don't like being called an older woman. Despite my wrinkles and flapping underarms, I'm a mere babe compared to my friend, Miss Ludie, now 96 years old. Second, the phrase "reverent in behavior" (NASB) sounds like I'll never again be able to tuck my nightshirt in my shorts and go out in my yard to prune roses. Third, I have never gossiped maliciously, only with the best intent. Fourth, I'm definitely

---

[73] Scribner and Ellison, *Woman to Woman*, 12, italics added.

not enslaved to wine. (However, I have been known to down a full jar of marshmallow cream in less than two minutes when overcome by a sugar craving.) Last, I'll be glad to teach what is good. Just give me an outline of what that includes and a mild sedative 30 minutes before I speak. And could you give me a podium that's high enough for me to rest my chin if I feel faint?

Many times I don't feel qualified to mentor. The problem is that by the time I do feel qualified I'll be in heaven with the Lord. While that's great for me, that doesn't do much for Mary Smith down here on earth looking for someone to help her grow.[74]

I am sure that the authors of this book are very nice people. And I rejoice in the fact that God has likely used them in ministry in many ways. As you read any book on ministry or the Christian life, however, you should always be attuned to what the authors' words say about their view of Scripture. Do their words show a high regard for the Word of God? Do their words promote the authority of Scripture and the glory of God? Do they embrace God's standards as their own? Are they willing to use Scripture as a tool for entertaining the reader? I am concerned that these authors convey in their words above a disregard for both the Word of God and the God of the Word. Can any devoted follower of Jesus have a bone to pick with the Author of Titus 2? In an effort to entertain, have these women not inadvertently made a mockery of Scripture?

The next section comes under the heading, "Qualified and Called." Here, the authors address the issue of qualifications:

When 189 Christian women in Virginia were surveyed regarding *what they wanted* in leaders, the top four prized characteristics were: commitment, love and trust of God, Christ and others, dedication to God and the church, compassion and caring. As you *reflect on these* characteristics, *consider* what qualifies you to serve as a mentor. *Read the following and check the ones which apply to you.*[75]

---

[74] Ibid., 12–13, italics added.
[75] Ibid., 13, italics added.

The authors list eight ideas, and then continue:

How many did you check? *You are more qualified than you think.* Qualification does not come with educational degrees, age (necessarily), or other accomplishments. Instead *you are qualified in your heart.* Christ qualifies you because you are a witness to His presence and love within your life experiences. *Serving as a mentor doesn't imply that you are fully mature.* In fact you may have a mentor while you mentor someone else. Serving as an effective mentor means that you are open to Christ, learning and growing, and actively pursuing your own wholeness (maturity). *The greatest gift you can give your merea*[76] *is yourself,* given out of your fullness in Christ, not out of obligation or needing to prove something.[77]

Again, we have to ask whether this book embraces the Scriptures as "God-breathed" and authoritative when it comes to identifying qualifications for mentors. Or, do we know better? Unfortunately, these authors are not alone in their thinking. A similar approach is found in Connie Witt's *That Makes Two of Us,* as she sets out to simplify the task of mentoring and dismiss the need to take the qualifications of Titus 2:3 seriously, all the while saying, "This is what God says."[78]

---

[76] *Merea* is the word Scribner and Ellison use for mentee.

[77] Scribner and Ellison, *Woman to Woman,* 13, italics added.

[78] This begins in the preface as Witt writes, "I realized I didn't have to be at a certain level with certain criteria before God could use me. In fact, if there was a criteria being set, I was setting it not God. He was ready to use me at any time…It's easy, it's fun, it isn't time intensive, and best of all, it's how God designed discipleship and mentoring to be!" This same line of thinking continues throughout the book. What is the felt need that she is elevating over the Word of God (which actually does state His criteria clearly)? Her concern (and that of Gary Smalley in the foreword) is that older women may be scared off if there are too many requirements. She wants this to be "easy enough" for women to do. By her own admission, her own marks in discipleship and evangelism are low (even though, according to Scripture, this is what God left us here to do), but in her husband's words, she has "the gift of hang," the ability to hang out with younger women. Later in her book when she relates an example of this (p. 50), we see that she has encouraged a lost woman (who had a conscience and concern about dressing modestly) to find something "flirty" to wear on a date…and Witt seems pleased with this, and calls this

The starting point for any genuinely Christian approach to mentoring has to be Scripture. And without a willingness to submit ourselves to what God has said in His Word we will never be able to honestly call our approach biblical. One of the things that 2 Tim 3:16-17 teaches us is not only that Scripture comes from God and is very valuable, but also that it is *sufficient* for thoroughly equipping us for every good work (including mentoring!). This is why it is important to avoid needs-based approaches. Such approaches are driven by something other than the Word of God. In fact, the Word of God simply becomes a resource for helping me to become a better me, rather than the authority for how I live and serve God. Thus, books like *Organic Mentoring*, which is based on the felt needs of younger women revealed in surveys, do not point us to a solid foundation for biblical mentoring.[79] In saying that, and in sharing the examples above, I am not seeking to discredit particular women. I have, for example, significantly benefited from Sue Edward's first book, *Leading Women Who Wound*, and have recommended it to thousands. I sincerely thank God for how He has used her to bless and edify other women. I cannot, though, rejoice over what is proposed in *Organic Mentoring*. In this case, I think the authors appear to have unwittingly shown disregard for God's Word, and turned instead to conventional wisdom. This illustrates again just how easy it is for *any* of us to fall into this trap. It should serve as a warning to all of us. Without being securely tethered to the sure anchor of Scripture we will inevitably drift away from God's truth, standards, and purposes, and ultimately God's honor will be compromised.

Philosophy matters. It matters as we choose what topics to cover with our mentees, and perhaps even more, it matters as we decide how we will go about covering them. This is because while choosing topics wisely is important, it is even more important that we address each topic *biblically*, bringing Scripture to bear on each issue.

What each of us will propose as we compile a list of topics to cover and as we flesh out each of the seven topics of Titus 2 will flow directly out of our personal philosophy. Whether the model we adopt is one that embraces,

---

mentoring. Unfortunately, much of the thinking in this book reflects the very thinking from which godly older women are to call younger women back to their senses.
[79] Edwards and Neumann, *Organic Mentoring*.

tolerates, or rejects entertainment as a means of accomplishing the goals will matter, and whether it is Scripture-based or needs-based will also matter.

Chapter 12

MY LIST

That brings us to my list. What topics do I think are important to cover with mentees? In compiling my list, I have attempted to work from Scripture, seeking to address needs identified by God, following a discipleship model, and taking to heart the meaning of the word God used in Titus 2:4 to communicate the remedial nature of the task. My list is neither all-encompassing nor without flaws. It is simply offered as a biblically based resource from which you can draw as you compile your own list.

The topics can all be grouped under four headings: the gospel, love, cultivating godly character, and cultivating ministry skills. They could be studied over a fixed period of time or indefinitely until one of you is promoted to heaven! I will elaborate on just the first two topics.

THE GOSPEL

Preach the Word; be prepared in season and out of season; correct, rebuke and encourage—with great patience and careful instruction. (2 Tim. 4:2)

But in your hearts set apart Christ as Lord. Always be prepared to give an answer to everyone who asks you to give the reason for the hope that you have. But do this with gentleness and respect, keeping a clear conscience, so that those who speak maliciously against your good behavior in Christ may be ashamed of their slander. (1 Pet. 3:15-16)

First and foremost, I recommend covering three areas related to the gospel: understanding and explaining the gospel well, sharing the gospel with others effectively, and giving a personal testimony that glorifies God, that is, one that includes the gospel front and center. These are so crucial that I do not rush through them, but rather return to them over and over again until we are both satisfied, and my mentee is well prepared to do all three. At times this has taken many weeks.

Why would I choose to do this? Two reasons: training and getting back on track. It is a training exercise. We are starting at the beginning, laying a most important foundation. After a mentee has shared her testimony with me, we return to the topic again with some teaching on the purpose of a testimony, some evaluation of hers as she shared it previously, and some training in how to share an effective testimony that includes the gospel and clearly glorifies God. She may want to try again verbally right away using what she has learned or wait until the next week. Or perhaps I will ask her to prepare a written testimony for our next meeting time. Before she shares the second time (I sometimes do this even before the first time), I usually warn her that we are going to return to this over and over again until she can share a testimony "perfectly, in her sleep," so that she knows in advance that this is something we will be working on for a while. The goal is for her to be able to share her testimony comfortably, effectively, and confidently, even as she also shares it in dependence on God's Spirit each and every time.

We may work on her ability to clearly communicate what led her to make her decision, her experience in making it, and a description of exactly what it is that she decided to do. I have heard many first attempts at "testimonies" of conversion that did not make mention of Jesus at all! Others have highlighted or glorified the sins of their pre-salvation years. And still others have focused on their old life and salvation experience, but made no mention of how their life changed as a result of their conversion. This is one of the reasons I intentionally use the somewhat out-of-vogue term "testimony" rather than teaching mentees to "tell their story." The story we want them to tell is a story of how Jesus gloriously rescued them from sin and transformed their lives, and can do the same for others through the power of the gospel. Often it just takes a bit of instruction for a mentee to become aware of where she has wandered off course in sharing her testimony and to get her back on track again.

Throughout this time, we concurrently work on the content of the gospel itself. What does it really mean? Where is she clear and where does she need clarification or instruction? Again, you may be surprised how few Christians can clearly explain the biblical gospel.

Finally, we turn our focus to how to share the gospel with others. This may involve discussions, role-playing, or writing a letter. Sometimes the whole process goes very quickly; other times the exercise takes more time. This depends on each mentee's understanding of the gospel, her aptitude in grasping the purpose of the testimony, and her ability to explain clearly how a person comes to be a follower of Christ.

As was her habit, Macy came walking up the path cut through the foot-and-a-half-deep snow to our front door, wearing naught but canvas shoes on her feet. It was a matter of taste and style. She was a snowboarder and a dancer and not a fussy dresser. I opened the door a crack and didn't return her greeting with the customary hug. Instead I said, "I'm not interested. I know you've been talking about Jesus and religious things with all my neighbors, but I don't want to hear about it." Her puzzled expression quickly gave way to the laugh she reserved for awkward situations, and the next moment she jumped right in. I love her different laughs. Impromptu, we role-played a witnessing scenario at my front door, with me as "the unsuspecting unbeliever" and her sharing the gospel and answering my objections. The truth is that she was actually the unsuspecting one; but she was far from unprepared. We had spent weeks already working just a little at a time, at the start of each session, on her testimony, the gospel, and witnessing. Eventually I let her in, and in the warmth of the living room we debriefed.

MY LIST

The Gospel

Giving a Personal Testimony
Understanding and Explaining the
  Gospel Well
Sharing the Gospel Effectively

Love

Loving God
  •Maintaining a Vibrant
   Relationship with God
  • Lordship
Loving Others
  • Other Believers
  • The Needy
  • Our Own Husbands
    Submitting
    Honoring
    Helping
  • Our Own children
  • Our Enemies
Building Loving, Healthy
  Relationships
Using Your Home as a Place for
  Showing Love

Cultivating Godly Character

Good Sense and Self-Control
Purity
Kindness
Modesty
Wisdom
Humility
A Teachable Spirit
Gratitude
Forgiveness

Cultivating Ministry Skills

Acts of Kindness: Good Deeds
Acts of Service: Meeting Needs
Encouragement: Ministering to the
  Lonely or Discouraged
Leading a Bible Study
Caring for the Hurting
Visitation
Knowing and Using Your Gifts
Understanding Feminism and God's
  Design for Women

LOVE

Most genuine Christians understand that we are called to be loving people. Fewer, though, have stopped to reflect deeply on what this looks like in practice.

Loving God

We are commanded to love the Lord our God with all our heart (with our whole being). This broad goal can be addressed in many ways. The two ways that I have chosen to focus on in most of my mentoring sessions are maintaining a vibrant relationship with God by cultivating a healthy devotional life, and showing love for God through obedience, submission, confession, and repentance, which is basically submitting to Jesus' lordship. Each of these is subsequently broken down into more manageable and specific areas. Depending on your mentee, you might spend anywhere from one to several sessions on each topic. As previously mentioned, training her to have an effective devotional life is so critical that you may choose to briefly return to this subject intermittently for many months.

One of your first goals is to help your mentee to see her devotional life as her *lifeline*. A healthy consistent devotional life is necessary for mind renewal, for the empowering she needs for godly living, for direction and redirection, for realigning her priorities, and for increased love for God. At the very least, time in God's Word should include consistent Bible reading and meditation. It can also include Scripture memorization, taking notes from your reading, studying God's Word, and journaling to keep a record of what you are learning. You may recall from previous chapters that training your mentee in this area can include modeling, encouraging, supporting, providing accountability, and offering her opportunities to share what she is learning from time to time once this lifeline habit has been established.

In training your mentee in prayer, you may want to do some or all of the following:

- Teach her how to praise (without requests or thanksgiving).
- Teach her how to give thanks (without adding requests).
- Teach her how to intercede for others using Scripture.
- Teach her how to pray in agreement with someone else.
- Pray together.
- Pray for her regularly.
- Share personal requests with her and expect her to pray for you.

- Pray with her for people in each of your lives who are lost.
- Model surrender to God's will in your prayers.
- Pray with her for church and national leaders, news events, political situations.
- Pray with her for specific missions requests.

Loving the Lord your God with all your heart also necessitates obedience and submission to His will. This is what the lordship of Jesus Christ is all about. Your mentee may have fallen prey to the mistaken notion that Christ-followers must choose between a focus on rules or relationship, implying that love and obedience are two different things. Jesus Christ Himself tells us clearly and repeatedly in the Gospel of John that we actually *demonstrate* our love for God *by* obeying His rules. "If you love me, you will obey what I command" (John 14:15). It is essential for your mentee to understand this; if she does not, she will not be able to obey the command to love God. Helping her to see this is helping her to get back on track.

> We actually demonstrate our love relationship with God by obeying His rules.

Recognize that this will take time. Allowing one week on this will not be sufficient. Submission is a difficult thing for most of us. It entails relinquishing our desire to be in charge and to have things our way. It means doing what someone else has determined instead of what we want to do. Or it can mean refraining from doing what we want to do or getting what we want to have. Full obedience is our lifetime job as followers of Christ. Helping your mentee get (or continue to build on) a good start on this is a very worthy endeavor.

Another factor in lordship is confession and repentance. As long as we live in our earthly bodies we will be susceptible to temptation. When we succumb and sin, both confessing our sin and turning away from it are essential for restoring our relationship with God. No matter who else we may have sinned against, every sin we are guilty of, whether by commission or omission, is a sin against God. Genuine repentance is demonstrated by a change in actions. Good intentions are not enough. Confession and repentance is the pathway to experiencing personal revival. A deepening relationship with God is impossible without them. We need to ensure that our mentees understand these things so they can grow in their love for God.

Loving Others

If the first major set of topics related to love can be summed up in the command to love the Lord our God with all our hearts, then the second can be summarized by the command to love our neighbors as we love ourselves. Under this heading I place loving specific others, building healthy and loving relationships, and using our home as a place to show love.

We are first told to love our neighbor as ourselves in Leviticus 19:18. This is quoted three more times in the Gospel of Matthew alone, as well as in Romans, Galatians, and James. Contrary to another common misconception, nowhere in Scripture are we encouraged to love ourselves; rather, the Scripture just mentioned implies that this is something we already do. Our evident concern for our own health, well-being, reputation, image, comfort, and much more all confirm this. It is time to intentionally move on. As Christian women, we are commanded specifically to love:

- Other believers: "Love one another deeply, from the heart" (1 Pet. 1:22). This command is ubiquitous in New Testament books such as the Gospel of John, 1 and 2 John, Romans, Galatians, Ephesians, and Hebrews.
- The needy: "He who despises his neighbor sins, but blessed is he who is kind to the needy" (Prov. 14:21); "He who oppresses the poor shows contempt for their Maker, but whoever is kind to the needy honors God" (Prov. 14:31); "Religion that God our Father accepts as pure and faultless is this: to look after orphans and widows in their distress and to keep oneself from being polluted by the world" (James 1:27).
- Our own husbands: "Then they can train the younger women to love their husbands" (Titus 2:4). This will include submitting to, honoring, and helping our husbands, as well as being their

friends and companions. "Wives, submit to your husbands as to the Lord" (Eph. 5:22). "The wife must respect her husband" (Eph. 5:33). "Neither was man created for woman, but woman for man" (1 Cor. 11:9; see also Gen. 2:19-25; 1 Cor. 7:2-5). These are all ways of showing love.

- Our own children: "Then they can train the younger women to love their...children" (Titus 2:4). A willingness to first *have* children may actually need to be taught to some mentees.

- Our enemies: "Do not seek revenge or bear a grudge against one of your people, but love your neighbor as yourself. I am the LORD" (Lev. 19:18). In Matthew 5:43-48, Jesus begins by quoting this passage from Leviticus and then expands its application: if we are to be perfect like our new adoptive Father in heaven, we must now love our enemies.

Given the breadth of Scripture's calls to love, I have made the assumption that all others who come into our lives should be recipients of our love. This includes those who are in our lives long-term through no choice of our own, such as a boss, relatives, a roommate, work associates, neighbors, and friends; and it includes those who cross our paths briefly, such as the woman selecting mushrooms next to us in the grocery store or waiting with us for a bus, a plane, or a doctor's appointment.

Because the idea of loving one's self has become so popular today, this is definitely an area that a wise mentor will want to broach with her mentee as she seeks to ensure that she is on track.[80] If she is not, the loving mentor will call her attention back to scriptural teaching on the matter and help her escape the world's influence and come to her senses. She will guide her mentee away from love of self or love of the world, which is usually just another version of self-love, and will refocus

---

[80] When God's Word commands us to love our neighbor as ourselves, it is not talking about a supposed need to have healthy self-esteem before we can love other people. It is calling us to care for the needs of others just as we care for our own needs. When we're hungry we feed ourselves; when others are hungry we should feed them. Although there are certainly some people who have too low a view of themselves because of how they have been treated or abused in the past, the vast majority of people have too high of a view of themselves.

her attention on loving God and loving others. This category of loving others is huge. It will take a lifetime to perfect.

Building Loving, Healthy Relationships
One way to address loving all these categories of people is by first discussing what it means to love generally, and then focusing on each specific group, considering how we can actively demonstrate love in each case. Practical application and accountability will be an integral part of this.

The world has many ideas about how to build healthy relationships, and some of these can be helpful. However, you will want to be sure to only include ideas that do not contradict biblical principles, either overtly or subtly. It is also worth making the effort to clearly identify what is biblical and what is not, not because there is no value in anything outside of Scripture, but because extra-biblical principles do not carry the same wisdom, promises, or power as God's inspired Word. This is reason enough to make the distinction, but additionally, as your mentee observes you doing this, it will also help her to grow in becoming more discerning as well.

Using Your Home as a Place for Showing Love
As we think about how to use our homes as a place for showing love, some of the subjects I have discussed with mentees include domesticity, stretching money, showing hospitality, entertaining *for God's glory*, and celebrating holidays in a meaningful way.

Domesticity covers being busy at home...and loving it! It has to do with making a house a home, creating a close sense of family, and caring for your household. Our primary responsibility will be to our family members, whether that is an aging parent, a husband, a child, a handicapped sibling, or a housemate. There is also incredible potential to extend beyond these as well.

The kitchen is the center of many homes. Food is not just necessary for life; it is an amazing gift from God in another sense: it allows us to show love to others. How a home is maintained also matters. Not everyone feels most at home in the same environment, but some environments preclude peace and harmony, comfort, or even the ability to think, while others promote these things. Not everyone will have the same appreciation of beauty, or a need for the same degree of cleanliness or organization, but we all know when limits have been reached. It may seem to be only a fine line that is crossed from a place where we thrive to a place we can only tolerate to a place where we feel pushed beyond our limits. The way our home is kept can elicit warmth and appreciation or discomfort, restlessness, and the desire to escape. Caring for one's family by providing meals, clean clothing, and a clean, safe, and well-ordered home are all ways of showing love. If you have any doubt, just reflect on the effects of the reverse. In situations where things like dirty clothes, lack of food, or a house that is filthy or in disrepair are completely avoidable, allowing these conditions to persist does not communicate love.

Stretching money involves being a good steward, caring for our families responsibly, and budgeting to find funds for family outreach and ministry. Regarding this last point, what is not spent on indulging ourselves can be used to show love to others. Some mentees will have to work harder at this than others. We may also need to point out to some that saving just to have more with which to indulge ourselves at a later time is not the goal here.

Showing hospitality is not the same as entertaining. It usually involves sacrificially meeting the needs of others as those needs are made known to you, often when it is very inconvenient to meet them. It often requires flexibility. It is still seen and needed today, though not as often in our society as it is in other cultures, or as it was in Bible times.

This gives you an idea of how I flesh out the topics on my list. While the list is clearly not exhaustive, it is still a comprehensive Matthew 28:20-type master list. If you are familiar with the seven "short list" topics of Titus 2, you probably recognized them tucked here and there into this broader list. Please keep in mind that this is not a checklist. It is shared as a resource for your consideration. In well over a decade of mentoring, I have never taken any one mentee through all of these topics.

What one mentor may place as a lower priority for her mentee, another may find indispensable or urgent. As you plan for what topics you will focus on and the order in which you will address them, continue to seek God's guidance. Allow His Holy Spirit to lead you in each and every decision. He does this in all sorts of ways. For instance, once after meeting for the better part of a year, one of my mentees expressed a desire to be taught about increasing her faith. This led to us exploring this subject for a number of weeks together. A mentee's needs and requests can often provide the impetus to a valid topic to study.

To recap, having a clear understanding of the intentional training aspect of mentoring, the corrective "getting back on track" nature of the call to the older women in Titus 2, and the role of accountability over the long haul will significantly impact how we go about choosing the topics we will cover with our mentees, the order in which we will cover them, and how we will cover them. Whether you use the seven topics listed in Titus 2 as your complete "curriculum," use a list like that of John Wesley and seek to intentionally combat common sins, create a list of topics based on your own life experiences, or use my "master list" as a starting point, the key is to be intentional. Genuine biblical mentoring does not just happen by osmosis as you hang out with your mentee.

CONCLUDING THOUGHTS:
WINDING DOWN, GEARING UP

As we wind down our discussion of the foundations of biblical mentoring, I want to emphasize the importance of knowing God's Word well. This must be your starting point. If the Scriptures do not set the direction for how your mentoring will be approached and for all that you will do, your mentoring will never be biblical. Your foundation is comprised of your thoughts, beliefs, and philosophy, and together these will set the tone and chart your course. If those thoughts, beliefs, and philosophy are not grounded in the Word of God, you cannot expect to have God use you to help a younger woman become more like Jesus. If you start out on the wrong trajectory, even just one degree off, the farther you go, the farther you will end up from the true standard. The longer you keep going on that track, the greater will be your divergence from the truth.

There is no shortage of ideas about how to get started in mentoring. We cannot, however, just "get started." The foundation that you will build on as you begin is critical. First we must lay a solid biblical foundation. That has been the goal of this book. Following that we must invest in personal preparation. Some help for doing this is provided in *Staying on Track: Equipping Women for Biblical Mentoring*. Then, we will be able to get started, because *then* the rest will fall into place—and when it does, we will be right on track.

Bobbie's growth in biblical discernment had been developed through her own study of God's Word, Bible classes at her church, and the Cypress Hills Ministries Women Mentoring Women workshop. One evening, as she sat in her church small group and listened, she realized that what was being affirmed had no biblical basis. When she had the opportunity to give input she simply responded, "Not everyone believes that." This really disturbed one man in particular. Zack strongly reaffirmed the idea, and a lively discussion ensued. A week later, Bobbie spoke with Zack again. She learned that back when he had been taught the problematic idea, he had accepted it without question, and it had been deeply ingrained in him. Having it called into question now had really troubled him. He had gone home after their last small group discussion and spent six hours wrestling with it and searching the Scriptures for himself. He eventually came to the conclusion on his own that there was indeed no biblical basis for what he had been led to believe all those years.

Even though he had an open mind and wanted to believe the truth, it had been a challenging and somewhat turbulent experience for Zack. When we believe something, and even more so when it has been our view for a long time, we become attached to it. In a sense, it becomes a part of who we are. Letting go can be difficult at best and traumatic at worst.

We have covered a lot of ground since the start of this journey together. Perhaps some of your previously held ideas have been challenged. Perhaps you have been challenged to be more careful about the foundation on which you are building your life and ministry. Perhaps you have committed to become a better Berean woman, or to be more intentional about having your life matter for eternity. I hope you are more determined now to build with materials that will last (1 Cor. 3:10-15), especially as you embrace God's call to mentor younger women.

We have covered a lot and it takes time to process it all. Allow yourself the time you need. Reflect, ponder, and seek God. Study the Scriptures on these points for yourself. Make up your mind. But after you have come to your conclusions, don't just sit back and rest. Keep moving towards the goal. The journey is not yet over. The next step in getting back on track is the training you will receive in *Staying on Track: Equipping Women for Biblical Mentoring.* God willing, we'll be talking again soon.

APPENDIX A:
MORE HELPFUL CHARACTER
TRAITS FOR MENTORS

Nine character traits from Donna Otto:[81]
1. A heart for God
2. A teachable spirit
3. God's perspective on time
4. A solid knowledge of her faith
5. Ability and boldness to share her beliefs
6. Commitment to people
7. Warm hospitality
8. Loving availability
9. An accepting affirming spirit

---

[81] Donna Otto, *Between Women of God: The Gentle Art of* Mentoring (Eugene, OR: Harvest House, 1995), 147–156. She calls these "The Fingerprint of God" on the older women; I love this.

Four character traits from Crawford Loritts:[82]
1. Brokenness
2. Uncommon communion
3. Servanthood as an identity
4. Radical, immediate obedience

Seven Attributes of Best Mentors from Regi Campbell:[83]
1. Maturity
2. Faith
3. Goodhearted
4. Confident
5. Dependent on God
6. Wisdom
7. Perseverance

Ten Necessary Traits for a Mentor from Gail MacDonald:[84]
1. Has devotion to Christ and building His kingdom
2. Is dependable
3. Is sensitive to others
4. Keeps short accounts in relationships
5. Lives as a steward, not an owner of things or people
6. Has suffered or failed and used it for growth
7. Is generous with honest affirmation
8. Shows mouth control
9. Has an active prayer life
10. Has "listening teachability"

---

[82] Crawford Loritts, "Four Traits of a Leader." Online: www.reviveourhearts.com/ articles/four-traits-leader/. Accessed June 17, 2013.

[83] Regi Campbell, *Mentor Like Jesus* (Nashville, TN: B&H, 2009), 145–147.

[84] Gail MacDonald, "Chapter Nine: Mentoring Woman to Woman," in *Heart to Heart with Pastors' Wives*, ed. Lynne Dugan (Ventura, CA: Regal, 1994), 101.

APPENDIX B:
GROUP MENTORING

The following are just a sampling of some contemporary models of group mentoring.

1. Betty Huizenga, *Apples of Gold* (Colorado Springs, CO: David C. Cook, 2000). Huizenga's approach involves small groups and combines cooking, eating, and Bible Study. It runs for six weeks, and the curriculum is provided. There are two special meals, one with spouses.
2. Regi Campbell, *Mentor like Jesus* (Nashville: B&H, 2009). Campbell's approach involves groups of eight, some apply to participate and some are handpicked. They meet for three hours monthly for a year, and also gather for retreats, one-on-one times, and times as couples with Regi and his wife. The focus is on reading and discussing key books, lots of accountability, Bible memorization, and personal reflection.

3. Donna Green, *Growing Godly Women: A Christian Woman's Guide to Mentoring Teenage Girls* (Birmingham, AL: New Hope, 2002). Green's approach involves groups of girls. All are welcome, and participants are encouraged to invite their friends. Very young "graduates" of the program are recruited to leadership. The approach combines social activities, Bible study, and values training. It also features an annual retreat.

4. Wayne Cordeiro, *The Divine Mentor* (Bloomington, MN: Bethany House, 2007). Cordeiro's approach involves groups meeting together in public places to have personal devotions and then to share what they have learned. Groups are not constant, with those participating sometimes changing from day to day. There is a clear outline of how the hour is spent.

5. Mary Lou Whitlock, "Chapter Ten: A Proposal for Preparation," in *Heart to Heart with Pastors' Wives*, ed. Lynne Dugan (Ventura, CA.: Regal, 1994). Available Online: www.ccel.us/hearttoheart. toc.html. Whitlock outlines a one-year program for seminary wives, "Mrs. in Ministry," that meets weekly, seminar style, utilizing guest speakers and experts. It includes some studies together and some social events.

6. Donna Otto, *Between Women of God* (Eugene, OR.: Harvest House, 1995), 171. Otto presents a "Mentors and Moms Program" in which the leader teaches on a topic and pairs of mentors and mentees listen together, discuss the content together, and hold each other accountable.

7. Gail MacDonald, "Chapter Nine: Mentoring: Woman to Woman," in *Heart to Heart with Pastor's Wives*, ed. Lynne Dugan (Ventura, CA: Regal, 1994), 97. Available Online: www.ccel.us/ hearttoheart.toc.html. MacDonald highlights Linda Anderson's "Mom to Mom program" (Grace Chapel, Lexington, MA). In this program, "older mothers take younger mothers under their wings for a year. In small groups, they discuss the biblical principles they were taught from a lecture Linda gives each week."

8. Anne Ortlund, "Chapter Eight, Discipling: Catch the Vision," in *Heart to Heart with Pastor's Wives*, ed. Lynne Dugan (Ventura, CA:

Regal, 1994), 90–92. Available Online: www.ccel.us/hearttoheart. ch8.html. Ortlund disciples young women in small groups of five or six for ten months only. There is a strong emphasis on reproduction and impacting the church from the inside out. Her former disciples once tracked down 600 women who had either been former disciples of hers or had been "discipled by someone who had been discipled by someone who had been discipled by her." Her approach is selective and focused on investing in future leaders.

9. "Seminary Wives Institute" at Southern Baptist Theological Seminary. The idea with this institute is similar to "Mrs. in Ministry," described above, but this is a three-year program with specific required and elective courses offered for credit. There are required assignments and fees for classes. Various certificates may be earned. See www.sbts.edu/wp-content/uploads/sites/12/2012/03/swi-brochure.pdf.

APPENDIX C:
LONG-DISTANCE MENTORING

Long-distance mentoring lends itself more naturally to the session approach than to the modeling approach. Sometimes mentoring takes place long-distance because of a lack of available mentors within close proximity. Other times it is chosen because the relationship between a mentor and her mentee has already been established and is fairly strong, and then one or the other needs to relocate. In the first century, Paul practiced long-distance mentoring with Timothy and Titus using letters. Today we have many methods for carrying out long-distance mentoring:

- letters
- email
- instant messaging
- phone
- video chat (Skype, FaceTime)

I have had the joy and privilege of participating in a variety of long-distance mentoring relationships over the years. My first experience with this was through regular weekly Skype meetings with my daughter-in-law-to-be. After a few years break, after she and our son had been married for three years, she asked if we could do this again; and we resumed our weekly "meetings." I have also used Skype for more occasional mentoring. This began when I was traveling and needed to miss some scheduled group mentoring sessions. That group mentoring arrangement has long since concluded, but I continue to mentor others on a more occasional basis over Skype even now.

I have also found the use of phone calls and email valuable for distance mentoring. Although my first preference is generally to interact in person or using Skype where we can both benefit from seeing one another, I recognize that this visual contact is less important for some people. In fact, for some, being able to organize their thoughts into writing is a huge advantage of distance mentoring. They also relish having comments in written form so that they can revisit, reflect on, and continue to digest what has been shared long after the conversation is over. I have found that most human beings, myself included, have a tendency to meet certain kinds of correction or negative feedback with defensiveness initially, but later find that they are able to be more receptive or responsive, even if that "later" is only a few moments after the initial confrontation. Mentoring via letters or other written communication provides this advantage naturally. It also allows for a natural and easy way to trace the progress of the mentee over time.[85]

UNIQUE PROTOCOLS

Unique protocols for distance mentoring arrangements begin with privacy considerations. Take care to ensure no one else can unintentionally hear your conversation due to speaker phones or Skype calls that are conducted through computer speakers rather than headsets. For Skype and phone calls you will need to consider time differences and suitable

---

[85] This is skillfully portrayed by Tim Cooper and Kelvin Gardiner in *Pastoring the Pastor* (Scotland, UK: Christian Focus, 2012), a creative account of an experienced pastor mentoring a novice largely by means of email.

meeting places on both ends of the conversation as well. Privacy and freedom from interruptions are just as important as if you were meeting in person, so they need to be ensured at both locations.

Finally, develop the habit of not forwarding an email thread between yourself and your mentee (or any other individual for that matter) to a third party without prior consent. This is a violation of their privacy and confidentiality and can very quickly erode trust.

ADVANTAGES

There are both advantages and disadvantages to long-distance mentoring. Access to someone particularly qualified or suited to mentoring you is a huge advantage. Continuing a well-established relationship with a strong foundation of love and trust already established is another. In a newly forged relationship it could be an advantage that no one close by knows the individuals that the mentee may be struggling to relate to, such as a friend, spouse, child, co-worker, boss, fellow church member, or even church leader. This safeguards the mentor against being drawn into taking sides or being tempted to think less of the individual or treat them poorly herself.

DISADVANTAGES

There are obviously many limitations to long-distance mentoring as well. You can't hug your mentee for one! And when she is hurting or lonely, or even in times when she is elated, that can be a real loss. If using phone or email rather than some form of video chat, you will also be unable to see one another's body language and facial expressions. This is a definite disadvantage, when you are discussing emotional, sensitive, or complicated issues, as a large percent of communication is transmitted through nonverbal means. At best, this void can translate into a real hindrance to communication; at worst, it can actually fuel miscommunication.

Sometimes we may feel like our lives are so filled with those who are close by that we cannot possibly make room for one more person, let alone a mentee who is on the other side of the country or the world. If God clearly leads you to mentor long-distance, you can trust Him to empower you to do it. A number of remarkable books of the New Testament were written as letters from one mentor to his mentee. Perhaps the record of your long-distance mentoring relationship will someday bless others too.

BIBLIOGRAPHY

Barsness, A. Jean. *Anywhere, Anytime, Any Cost: Can I Trust God with My Zip Code?* Winnipeg, MB: Word Alive, 2013.

Bridges, Jerry. Foreword to *Walking Like Jesus Did: Studies in the Character of Christ* by Larry McCall. Winona Lake, IN: BMH Books, 2005.

Campbell, Regi. *Mentor Like Jesus.* Nashville, TN: B&H, 2009.

Christenson, Evelyn. "Grace for Aging." Online: www.reviveourhearts. com/radio/revive-our-hearts/grace-aging/.

Cooper, Tim and Kelvin Gardiner. *Pastoring the Pastor.* Scotland, UK: Christian Focus, 2012.

Cordeiro, Wayne. *The Divine Mentor.* Bloomington, MN: Bethany House, 2007.

Edwards, Sue and Kelley Matthews. *Leading Women Who Wound: Strategies for an Effective Ministry.* Chicago, IL: Moody, 2009.

Edwards, Sue and Barbara Neumann. *Organic Mentoring.* Grand Rapids, MI: Kregel Ministry, 2014.

Elliot, Elisabeth. *Through Gates of Splendor.* Carol Springs, IL.: Tyndall House, 2005.

Fryling, Alice. *Disciplemakers' Handbook.* Downers Grove, IL: IVP, 1989.

Green, Donna. *Growing Godly Women: A Christian Woman's Guide to Mentoring Teenage Girls.* Birmingham, AL: New Hope, 2002.

Grubb, Norman. *C. T. Studd, Cricketer and Pioneer.* London: Lutterworth, 1995.

Hendricks, Howard and William Hendricks. *As Iron Sharpens Iron: Building Character in a Mentoring Relationship.* Chicago, IL: Moody, 1995.

Huizenga, Betty. *Apples of Gold: A Six-Week Nurturing Program for Women.* Colorado Springs, CO: David C. Cook, 2000.

Kraft, Vicky and Gwynne Johnson. *Women Mentoring Women: Ways to Start, Maintain and Expand a Women's Ministry.* Chicago: Moody, 2003.

Loritts, Crawford. "Four Traits of a Leader." Online: www.reviveourhearts.com/articles/four-traits-leader/.

Louw, Johannes P. and Eugene A. Nida, eds. *Greek-English Lexicon of the New Testament Based on Semantic Domains.* (2 vols. Second edition. New York: United Bible Societies, 1988, 1989.

Lowry, Lois. *The Giver.* New York: Laurel Leaf, 2002.

Luck, Ulrich. "σωφρονίζω." Page 1104 in vol. 7 of *Theological Dictionary of the New Testament.* Edited by G. Kittel and G. Friedrich. Translated by G. Bromiley. 10 vols. Grand Rapids: Eerdmans, 1964-76.

MacDonald, Gail. "Chapter Nine, Mentoring: Woman to Woman," in *Heart to Heart with Pastor's Wives,* ed. Lynne Dugan. Ventura, CA: Regal Books, 1994.

Mayhall, Carole. *Words That Hurt, Words That Heal: Speaking the Truth in Love.* Colorado Springs, CO: NavPress, 2007.

Muller, George. *The Autobiography of George Muller.* New Kensington, PA: Whitaker House, 1985.

Ortlund, Anne. "Chapter Eight, Discipling: Catch the Vision," in *Heart to Heart with Pastor's Wives,* ed. Lynne Dugan. Ventura, CA: Regal Books, 1994.

Otto, Donna. *Between Women of God: The Gentle Art of Mentoring.* Eugene, OR: Harvest House, 1995.

Otto, Donna. *Finding a Mentor, Being a Mentor.* Eugene, OR: Harvest House, 2001.

Peace, Martha. *Becoming a Titus 2 Woman.* Bemidji, MN: Focus, 1997.

Pearl, Michael and Debi Pearl. *To Train Up A Child.* Pleasantville, TN: No Greater Joy Ministries, 2002.

Robertson, A. T. *A Grammar of the Greek New Testament in the Light of Historical Research.* Nashville: Broadman, 1934.

Scribner, Tricia and Edna Ellison. *Woman to Woman: Preparing Yourself to Mentor.* Birmingham: New Hope, 2011.

Stuart, Douglas and Gordon Fee. *How to Read the Bible for All Its Worth.* Grand Rapids, MI: Zondervan, 2003.

Towner, Philip H. *The Letters to Timothy and Titus.* NICNT; Grand Rapids: Eerdmans, 2006.

Van Allsburd, Chris. The Polar Express. Boston, MA: HMH Books for Young Readers, 1985.

Van Atta, Lucibel. *Women Encouraging Women: Who Will Disciple Me?* Colorado Springs, CO: Multnomah Press, 1987.

Wesley, John. *On the Education of Children,* Sermon 95. Online: www.umcmission.org/Find-Resources/John-Wesley-Sermons/Sermon-95-On-the-Education-of-Children.

Whitlock, Mary Lou. "Chapter Ten: A Proposal for Preparation," in *Heart to Heart with Pastors' Wives,* ed. Lynne Dugan. Ventura, CA: Regal, 1994.

Witherington, Ben. "Love --as Defined by Children." Online: http://benwitherington.blogspot.ca/2007/10/love-as-defined-by-children.html.

Witt, Connie and Cathi Workman. *That Makes Two of Us.* Loveland, CO: Group, 2009.

An Invitation

WOMEN MENTORING WOMEN WORKSHOPS

Cypress Hills Ministries Women Mentoring Women Workshops offer women a learning context that is both interactive and reflective, combining practical exercises with in-depth biblical teaching that is designed to help women review, process, and internalize key concepts and engage in self-evaluation and preparation for mentoring. Participants enjoy times of rich fellowship as they engage in prayer times, group assignments, discussions, and conversations over meals. Visit cypresshillsministries.com for more information on upcoming workshops or contact CHM to inquire about scheduling a workshop in your area:

contact@cypresshillsministries.com

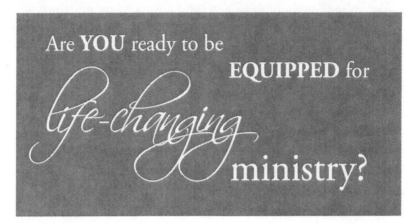

STAYING ON TRACK
by Jo-Anna Culy

ISBN:978-1-4866-1045-7

Now that you've come to understand what biblical mentoring is all about, *Staying on Track* will guide you as you take the next practical steps to become an effective mentor.